T0194696

TRUTH

— AND THE —

TRANSCENDENT BUSINESS

Heresy or Prophesy?

Dave Geenens

WESTBOW
PRESS®
A DIVISION OF THOMAS NELSON
& ZONDERVAN

CONTENTS

CONTENTS

ADMIRATION AND PRAISES

"Truth and the Transcendent Business is a must read for the serious Christian businessperson and any earnest person trying to deeply understand the beauty and responsibility of business leaders in free market economies. Our sound-bite culture offers few meaningful solutions to the growing socio-economic divide in the American economy. This book provides a clear and convincing answer to the divide, along with a glimpse at what arguably fulfills The Lord's Prayer in the business dimension; 'on earth as it is in heaven.'"

Deacon Dana Nearmyer
Archdiocese of Kansas City in Kansas

"This book speaks to businesspeople and instructs that, what the secular world has held up as critical to a company's success, is in error. Yes, profit is essential for a business to exist, but it is not the reason for its existence. Business is about service, and that service must include concern for all stakeholders. Investors are entitled to a return, but so are employees. Finding the proper balance is the inspired challenge of this book. Those hostile to a Judeo/Christian worldview will be both challenged and intrigued by the role perfected virtue plays in the protection of free markets and business excellence."

John L. Menghini
Retired President, Gear for Sports, Inc.

"Dave Geenens has, again, demonstrated how to blend faith with business; something that very few leaders can or actually do in practice. I speak from personal experience having been a top executive at Enron for 23 years. Ken Lay always said that he wanted Enron to be a place where everyone was able to use their God-given talents to achieve more than they ever believed they could. I experienced that dream of Lay's, as did many of Enron's former 25,000 employees. I continue to search for leaders that this describes; ones whose faith is strong, deep, and lived for the benefit of all people."

Cindy Olson
Founder, Executive Strategic Alliance

"Can a career in business help you get to heaven? Is it possible to transcend the vagaries of modern business in order that our efforts may have both practical and eternal significance? Dave Geenens provides answers, demonstrating the solid theory behind transcendent business along with practical examples of its application. Read, learn, apply – and you'll be grateful from now to eternity."

Kevin Lowry
CFO, RevLocal, LLC

"Truth and the Transcendent Business is more than a good read. It's an informing and inspirational treatise demanding your attention. As the tide of government intervention encroaches evermore rapidly on freedom and liberty, Dave's insights, gleaned from history and the present, give foundational teaching to those leaders who dare consider how our Christian faith must integrate with business. Let me warn you, his thesis is uncomfortable. Why? Because the content of the book forces us (Christians) to consider how we will live the truth and the expectation to transcend while in the workplace."

Charles (Chuck) McGuire
Former COO, Avascend Healthcare Hospitality

"Everyone, especially young people, want to make an impact on the world. We're doing everyone a disservice if we don't teach them and remind them of what our duties as Christians are – especially in our work. This book spells out the importance of the intersection between our faith and business. It provides the reader with both academic and virtuous examples of how a free market can function optimally when our faith shines forth in beliefs, values, paradigms, and behavior. As both an educator and a monk as well as a former business executive, this book is a valuable reference for helping to connect our Sunday worship with our Monday work."

Father Luke Turner, OSB, MBA
Benedictine College – Atchison, KS

"Dave Geenens artfully and methodically analyzes economic theory, religious teachings, and business strategy in search of the true purpose of business. Very few have attempted, and even less succeeded in combining theory, philosophy, strategy, and application like he does here. The result is a powerful and penetrating exploration of why Truth is more at stake now than ever before. The beauty of *Truth and the Transcendent Business* is that it comes as a refresher for some and as an education for others, reminding us that the greatness of the world and of business are a function of the greatness and magnanimity of the individual."

Alec Haight
Vice President, Pioneer Music Company

DEDICATION

To _____

(Insert reader's name here)

In memory of Kimber Rose Lane
June 21, 2004 – January 10, 2021

Angels often come in tiny and humble forms.

ACKNOWLEDGMENTS

I will let history judge the significance of this writing, but for purposes of sharing credit for the content of this book and its potential, nothing like this is ever accomplished alone or in a vacuum. People ask me how long it takes to write a book. The actual writing time is about two years, plus-or-minus six months. The work to read, gather perspectives, data, facts, and listen to and develop arguments and thoughts? Several years, perhaps decades. I began to consider, study, and practice some of the concepts shared in this book over 30 years ago! Of course, much of the wisdom shared in this book is ancient and the invaluable insight of philosophers and obedient Christ-followers and practitioners.

Benedictine College as an academic institution and community must receive top billing for both the latitude, the indirect challenge, and the margin to do this work. There is not a day that goes by where I feel any friction between my teaching assignments, the mission of the College, and the work to make known timeless principles of business, management, and leadership consistent with the Christian faith. I hope all of you someday can experience the freedom of this alignment and purpose.

The writings of the Catholic Church on business to which you have or will be exposed in this book are vast and informative. It is the only place I know of where Christian wisdom and truth about commerce and business, fully aligned with Biblical principles, exists. The Church, while not offering specific solutions, refers to its social teaching as an "indispensable and ideal orientation.'" I agree.

Throughout my 11-plus years at Benedictine, students have challenged me to dive deeper and have joined me in both the research and the study of virtuous business leaders and their companies; some of which are included in the Virtuosos chapter in this book. As part of a student fellows program funded at the College over the last decade, the following student researchers have contributed meaningfully to the work in this book. A special thanks and blessings to all of you.

Eric Lampe	Gary Harrison	Ian O'Hagan
Paul Floersch	Molly Judd	Rachel Sutterer
Alec Haight	Robert Williams	Andrew Sorley
Chris Jones	Stephen Loosbrock	Luke Norville
Emily Kendrick	Kevin Browne	Paul Seaton
Lucas Aitchison	Sydney Dickson	Noah Sattler
Vince Hooley	Will Keiss	Andrew Seaton
Ryan Boh	Michael Pesely	Corey Hollis
Catherine Francois	Matthew Sluder	Greta Peterson
Jordan Francescon	Evelyn Wagner	Mary Redmond
Joseph Machado	Andrew Ochs (special mention)	

If any businesses or organizations are fortunate enough to employ any of these people, you have the best. Let them lead.

Thank you to Kelly Uran, Adrian O'Hara, Chuck McGuire, John Menghini, Father Luke Turner, Deacon Dana Nearmyer, Terese Aquino, Michael Twombly and many others who invested time reading and providing feedback and encouragement on early iterations of the manuscript leading to this book. A big thanks goes out to the Virtuoso companies and Christian leaders in this book who trusted us; giving us access to their most intimate values, paradigms, and beliefs in their business. Many more Virtuosos have trusted us. God willing, their amazing stories will populate future writings.

I extend my sincere appreciation to Therese Aquino for the cover art and layout, and to Michael Twombly for his professional photography.

As I complete this book, Benedictine College is embarking on a remarkable mission for the next 30-years: to transform the culture of America. Our moral rules and related cultural norms in the U.S. appear either lost or gone. I trust and hope in some way what is written in these pages, much of which has been written before but has either been forgotten or never read, makes it to the eyes and ears of Christian business leaders, with an eventual resting place in the hearts and minds thereof.

Hope informs me that all is not lost. We must all carry the light of Jesus Christ into the shade or shadows in which, too often, business resides. I hope and pray this book provides lasting oil for your lamps. Hasten the day.

PREFACE

I have had this debate with many on our campus. People expect a business school and its professors to teach and speak of the practice and disciplines of business to make a profit. It's the proverbial spots on a leopard. It's what we do and who we are. We cannot change. Likewise, people expect theologians and the religious to teach on and speak of God and his creation; mankind; their struggles, their temptations, and, eventually, their redemption and return to God as part of His divine plan for humanity.

When I completed my third book and began the search for a publisher, I was rejected more times than I care to mention. The book, *Nothing is Free – The Price Only Business Leaders Can Pay to Protect Free Markets*, fits in the realistic fiction genre and tells the story of a female CEO who learns the real purpose of business through taking her company public, the related pressures, and her faith journey. When soliciting publishers, I'd explain the book and send an advance copy. Their responses would go something like this: "Well, the book must either be a business book or a religion book. This is somewhere in between, so we do not see how this book fits into our portfolio. Sorry."

Apparently, religion editors within booksellers/publishers do not know what to do with a business book that speaks of the role faith plays in business, and business editors within the same do not know what to do with a religious book that speaks of business and how it impacts and leverages one's faith. Heresy on both fronts! Yet I dare acknowledge there is a hunger in the marketplace to reconcile one's faith with one's work for the sake of avoiding the continuous friction a Christian business leader feels between their worship on Sunday and their work on Monday. But the obstacles to seeing clearly how the Christian faith and business interface are numerous and substantial. For centuries, the arena of commerce has been deaf to the Church and its teachings and that silence left room for ideologies, beliefs, and paradigms that are reflected in business as it functions today. Absent another option or voice, are we doomed to practice business with profit as its primary motive and people as its means?

That is not God's plan. The writings of the Catholic Church related to economics, commerce, and business are both profound and prophetic during this time. I have found no other place or resource where the human person is central to the story of work and their spiritual well-being is the responsibility of those leading in business. The Church's tongue is sharp in its outright rejection of socialism/collectivism, and it is equally as sharp with its expectations of Christian business leaders to concern themselves with people working in a free-market business as ends in-and-of themselves; not merely means used to attain the end of profit.

At the end of the day, I wrote this book, not for the booksellers or publishers, but for the Christian business leader hungry for an essential and eternal motivation to pursue that to which they are called: business. The book dives deep into classical writings and philosophies from Adam Smith, whose wisdom and insights, especially those rarely published or illuminated, are valid today. Smith speaks of things the Church teaches as problems arising in a free market without religion and virtue.

At the end of the day, a free market functions well only when moral laws are lived and exhibited in the beliefs, values, paradigms, and behaviors of Christian business leaders. In fact, the preservation of our free-market economy and protection of liberty depends on Christian business leaders ascending to this prophetic role: leading transcendent businesses. And truth lights the way.

A Word of Caution

Before you continue, be aware that when the light of truth enters a room, it reveals the falseness and ugliness in the shadows and corners. It will reveal the folly of other options and often of the past. As we naturally mature and learn more, it is common to reflect on our years of experience and recognize past failures when exposed to the truth. This can result in feelings of regret and guilt. I experienced this when I was writing this book, having not known the truth during my early years as a business leader.

You will likely experience similar feelings when reading this book. The key is to not feel shame. The truth does not condemn, yet it does convict. The truth may sound like heresy at first and you may feel tempted to stop, but the light of truth and reason will prevail. My advice? Face forward. Stick with it. Listen with big ears, an open mind, and a soft heart. Think rationally about what is presented. This book is about prophecy; what you will do and see tomorrow and in the future; not what you did yesterday. Peace to you.

INTRODUCTION

In what many call a post-truth world, not only is truth subject to debate, but its mere existence is questioned. I am sorry to disappoint you if you believe truth does not exist - choices, actions, and life would be much easier if the friction of truth were not at play. Whether we are conscious of it or not, the truth does exist and is visible and experienced by us every day. For example, jump off a chair and on to the floor and let me know if the law of gravity is true. It's easy to accept this law as truth because we see and experience its truth along with other universal physical and natural laws daily, though often we are unconscious of them. Might the same hold true for moral laws? Is there such a thing, and if there is, might we be able to see the effect of and experience it in the same way?

Let's give it a try. Go take for your own the possession of another; say a tool, a cell phone, or a writing instrument. It is possible the person subject to your repossession or thievery never finds out, but how did you feel about doing this? Even if you did not do it – which I trust you didn't freely choose to do so – what kept you from doing it or what did you anticipate you would feel if you did? How might the person stolen from react? What might he or she think of you as the perpetrator of the theft? Did you feel guilt even thinking about it? Did you project remorse or regret? My guess is that what you felt or anticipated is very normal and consistent, if not universal with what others would feel; much like the law or truth of gravity. There would be a few who would experience little or no conscience about thievery, but most would feel otherwise. What is this natural predisposition to not take another's property? I would argue this consensus on feelings is evidence of some moral truth, and like physical and natural truths, we are often unconscious of it.

Why do people have no problem believing natural and physical truths, yet hesitate to acknowledge the existence of moral truth today? Much of this depends on one's worldview. If the order of the natural world was put in place by a Creator - versus being the product of a chaotic explosion in the universe from which man evolved from an amoeba - then is it possible that rules were set in place to govern the relationships of the Creator's most valuable and important creation, man and his relationship with other human beings, the products of the earth, and the fruit of his toil? If not from this worldview, then from where does man's conscience come? Is our conscience entirely self-serving and utilitarian as if we individually are the center of the universe; surrendering only when faced with a dilemma that could harm us personally?

We can liken moral truth to the keel of a ship. A ship's keel is not visible below the water line, but it is there and it serves an integral purpose; to keep the ship upright when severe winds and waves threaten its stability. In conjunction with a ship's rudder and engines, the ship's keel helps it maintain a steady and safe course to its ultimate destination.

> **The relative morality commonplace today, absent of moral truth, is like a set of sails that catch every nuanced breeze of influence and any large shifts in thinking act like waves on our hull to render our lives unstable.**

Lives that are not properly ordered and lack a sense of structure create instability and danger. We have power and we have direction, but our course changes drastically when the force of wind and water pound our vessel (our mind, body, and soul) even to the point of us listing, if not capsizing.

In business, I contend that this disorder and instability are even worse. Why so? The idea that the purpose of business is to maximize shareholder wealth has dominated the landscape of business for decades. This belief is so engrained now that the truth of business or any other remnant or recount of the true purpose of business is all but invisible. Like a ship's invisible keel below the water line, this does not mean the truth doesn't exist and that it's not important for both your journey as a business leader and for reaching your ultimate destination, that which is in-and-through business.

In his book, *Business as a Calling*, Michael Novak shares this:

> "First, business is a morally serious enterprise, in which it is possible to act either immorally or morally. Second, by its own internal logic and inherent moral drive, business requires moral conduct; and, not always, but with high probability, violations of this logic lead to personal and business disgrace."[2]

Moral behavior in business is a choice and that choice has significant consequences for the both the business actor or leader and his or her audience. Pope Francis calls the vocation of the businessperson "a noble vocation, provided that those engaged in it see themselves challenged by a greater meaning in life; this will enable them to truly serve the common good by striving to increase the goods of this world and to make them more accessible to all."[3] If you are reading into this some type of redistribution-of-wealth-strategy or socialist conspiracy, you'd be wrong. The Church unapologetically rejects the tenets of socialism, but, likewise, though to a lesser extent, rejects the idea of liberal or free market economics, except where Christian business leaders temper the trajectory and tendencies of those in a free market with prudence and justice, among other virtues.

> "The Church has long taught that the value of any economic system rests on the personal virtue of the

individuals who take part in it."[4] - Timothy Cardinal Dolan

You see, there is a truth about business and expectations of business leaders whether they are visible today or not. The truth about the purpose of business relates directly to mutually beneficial exchanges that meet needs and create value through a consequential concern for other people. Adam Smith spoke of this in this famous excerpt from his classic, *An Inquiry into the Nature and Causes of the Wealth of Nations (The Wealth of Nations)*, "It is not from the benevolence of the butcher, the brewer, or the baker that we expect our dinner, but from their regard to their own self-interest."[5] This quote is most often seen as a stand-alone commentary addressing the correlation between one's self-interest and an economic livelihood benefiting another. Why will people help others or trade value for value if they are outrageously selfish? Smith's answer is simple – my neighbor will help me to truck, barter, or trade with me if there is something in it for my neighbor.[6] I believe and experience this as truth.

But this quote is followed by this much-less-publicized sentence in Smith's *Wealth of Nations*, "We address ourselves not to their (the businessperson's) humanity but to their self-love, and never talk to them of our own necessities, but of their advantages."[7] Does this not ring your moral chime with a muted clunk?! Our primary interactions in a free market economic system are to stroke the self-love and egos of those with power over us?! Maybe it's the way I am wired, but I reject this notion because I will not and do not do this. That's not me, it's not right, and something significant is missing here.

> "While Smith did not see us (you and me) as saints, he saw us clearly."[8] – Russell Roberts

I suggest to you that Smith's source of morality, though considered by some as independent from the commercial sphere he wrote about in *The Wealth of Nations*, is perhaps causal to what many witness today as business done absent a moral keel.

What happens when the keel of morality is no longer functioning as it was intended; when these fixed set of rules set in place by our Creator are set aside and those with power can do what they want with those less powerful? We end up with some of the abuses in business we see today, and a revolutionary response is born; one that we have seen before in history and one that we hear knocking on the door of the U.S. economy and in political circles now. Democratic Senator Bernie Sanders from Vermont captured the imagination of millions of Americans with his social democratic message and populous revolution in the 2016 presidential election, and delivered the same, if not more radical socialist message in the 2020 presidential campaign debates.

> **I suggest to you that socialism is a response to something; a lagging indicator of injustice, if you will.**

We will explore the truth about socialism and the Church's perspective thereon in this book. Concern for and pursuit of social justice is good and worthy of all our best efforts, but the ultimate solution to remedying social injustice is absolutely **not** socialism.

The ancient wisdom of the Church has much to say about the truth of business. Does this surprise you? It certainly did me. The purpose of this book is to unveil this wisdom, its relevance today through other teachings, and its evidence in today's progressive management practices. We as business leaders listen to lots of people and voices: Simon Sinek, Warren Buffett, Gary Hamel, Bob Nardelli and many more. Why not listen to wisdom of the ages from sources interested in life beyond our vapor-like life here on this earth?

You may be wondering why the Church would speak so loudly into business. That is a fair question. Though the Church has long spoken on social justice through its history of Papal Encyclicals, the modern foundations for social justice and business were set out in what many consider the foundational Catholic Social Doctrine Encyclical Letter,

Rerum Novarum, written in 1891 by Pope Leo XIII. History informs us that Pope Leo XIII wrote this foundational encyclical on the heels of the atrocious working conditions found during the Industrial Revolution in Europe, where capitalists were frequently exploiting human beings in an environment of laissez-faire government and a lack of intervention into commerce, and the swell of a revolutionary response was brewing. The insight into business, commerce, and the human person in these writings is both instructional and profound, even today.

The concerns of Pope Leo and the popes to follow center on the human person, both the laborer and the capitalist. There are clear expectations of both that will surprise you, as these truths are rarely spoken of today. This concern for the human person in commerce leads us back to the idea of a Creator and the purpose of His creation, man. Man and woman were created to transcend the earth. We were created for a transcendent purpose; to love, serve, and eventually, return to God.

For all men and women to transcend, fixed moral laws – the truth set out in the beginning – must be part of your business equation. The practice of virtues must be part of the life of a business leader. In fact, I will reveal in this book what I believe is a governing dynamic in economics: the level of government intervention in the economy is inversely proportional to the level of virtue practiced in business. For those of us wishing to protect liberty, the right to private property, the dignity of the human person (in the economic sector), the pursuit of the common good, and for a solution to social injustice, this dynamic is critical to understand and act on.

Business leaders were made to transcend. Those working in business were made to transcend. A transcendent business creates an environment where people can flourish; not only materially, but spiritually. And the truth, so opaque and invisible today, must inform our business lives and our businesses to bring this transcendence about. The consequences of not pursuing transcendence in business are predictably worse than any Coronavirus or biohazard on the lives and livelihoods of all people.

> **Business is not just a force for good. That it is. But it is also a force for God!**

Need evidence? Simply look at the state and priorities of business today, the ignorance of the Church's teaching about business, the frequent hypocrisy visible from Christians leading business either by choice or out of ignorance, and the damage done to the Church when on-lookers see the incongruence of beliefs and actions at work. We will uncover in this book the more sinister side of pride that often unwittingly leads others away from God, for which we as Christian business leaders will answer.

When I say ignorance, I do not mean to offend. I, too, was ignorant until God captured my heart and mind for his work through business. When writing this book, one of my first big decisions was to determine whether we, as Christians, are uneducated about the truth and the transcendent business or if we are educated way beyond our obedience. I have chosen the former because, if not educated, we will never attain to that which is higher still and have the privilege and freedom of choice to obey.

Many business leaders when anticipating this truth automatically assume that they and their businesses will be less competitive, less innovative, too 'friendly' to optimize results, and worry about what the current preeminent stakeholder, the shareholder, will think of this idea. Again, this anxiety will prove to be ill-placed. The truth reveals this is not the case when we understand leadership in business at its core. Yes, you must give up something, but it has little to do with business and it is fully consistent with Holy Scripture.

As you proceed to read this book and explore the truth, I have one wish for you; it is to not fear. Commit to knowing and living the truth. Transcend and help others do so through your business. It's your calling as a business leader. Jesus came to bear witness to the truth. As a Christ-follower, the world needs you to be a witness to the truth in all aspects of your life, even in business; perhaps especially in business. May peace, courage, and the grace of our Lord Jesus Christ accompany your effort.

CHAPTER 1

Adam Smith's Folly

᠙᠑᠙᠑

BEFORE WE CAN TALK wisely about business leadership, we must address businesses, and before we address businesses, we must first understand the environment or market in which businesses function. It would be dishonorable to discuss and begin to consider understanding the course of free markets and liberty without giving Adam Smith his due and sharing the broader scope of his thoughts and insights. While many of us work in and benefit from businesses operating in a significantly free market in the U.S., few of us understand how we got here and what elements Smith identifies as critical and those of which he cautions that can cause the demise of free markets.

This chapter would likely offend Adam Smith, and the title is likely scandalous to those who study Smith, follow Smith, and those who run in free market circles. I would like to go on record, though, that I desire to shower Adam Smith with all the praise worthy a philosopher, writer, and prophet. His works through his written word are profound and reflect a deep understanding of the human person that at times amuse and astound (because they are so true). I use the word "folly" in the chapter title above because it has Biblical roots in the Old Testament book of Ecclesiastes written by Solomon – a man blessed with wisdom, and any heavier word like "flaw" implies too much error on Smith's part. Our modern form of economic activity is vastly different from that of Smith's time.[9] Anyone seeking what makes some nations greater economically than others in the 18th century would have scarcely been able to anticipate the speed of delivery and communications, the evolution of and integration of technology, and the deep financialization of the economy evident in business today. These developments alone would challenge profound theories like Smith's.

> **But Smith's truths, for the most part, have stood the test of time. And I contend, so too, has his folly.**

History records that Adam Smith and the Scottish philosopher David Hume were good friends and colleagues. It is not surprising then, that with some minor variations, Smith's theories reflect an understanding of man's reason consistent with Hume's. It is appropriate to provide a brief synopsis of some of Hume's thoughts that are core to Smith's theory of morality; what I believe to be a prerequisite to clearly understanding Smith's emphasis on self-interest and the benefit of free markets. It should be noted that Hume was considered an Atheist (though he never admitted to that and his final religious preference is unclear)[10], while Smith was considered a Deist (though he grew up the son of a devout Christian mother).[11] Their attempts to explain the natural behavior of man were informed by, but not clouded by religious orthodoxy or what many might refer to as spiritual compromise. This lends common sense and rational credibility to their work. This also sets the stage for faith to meet reason, consistent with Church teaching. What is meant here? Though faith is required to believe in things unseen, God's creations and rules are wholly consistent with natural law, which is both seen and rational – creating the space for faith and reason to reconcile. Hume's rationale evident in Smith's philosophies, and their congruence with what we experience and see through the Church's teachings, is where faith and reason meet.

Adam Smith and Hume's Justice

Hume purports that private benevolence is not the original motive for justice.[12] He argues that justice is not derived from nature, but from education and man's convention.[13] Though artificial, Hume believes the rules of justice are far from arbitrary; so much so that he even refers to them as the Laws of Nature or natural law.[14] Why such an emphasis on justice? Hume suggests, ". . . as no principle of the human mind is more natural than a sense of virtue; so no virtue is more natural than justice."[15] This concept is important as we seek to understand more about private property and the role of justice in commerce.

At the core of man's convention of justice is the ability to acquire and hold private property through one's own fortune and industry. In the U.S., we take earning, acquiring, and holding personal property like homes, cars, phones, computers, books and more for granted. We don't even consider another alternative! Hume contends that without the inequality that accompanies the pursuit and acquisition of private property, the concept of justice is unnecessary and void of substance.[16] Because we as human beings are given different gifts, skills, and learned capabilities and because we are born into different geographies and families, inequality is both evident and manifest.

Hume scoffs at the idea that man and animal have the same narrow passion for selfish pursuits without regard to anyone other than him or herself. Hume goes so far as to state, "When every individual person labours apart, and only for himself . . . he never attains perfection in any particular art . . . ."[17] He uses terms like "savage and solitary"[18] to describe this undesirable and infinitely selfish state of man. These themes are woven throughout Smith's work and, not surprisingly, this infinitely selfish state of man observed widely in the practice of business today is likely a consequence of Smith's yet-to-be-illuminated folly.

Hume argues that the peaceable state of society is dependent on rules that govern private property rights, the rise of justice and injustice, and the perceptions of others on how one concerns himself with his property and the property of others. "There is nothing, which touches us more nearly than our reputation, and nothing on which our reputation more depends than our conduct, with relation to the property of others."[19] He also contends that society is maintained by this mutual ability to attain private property, and to appreciate that ability in others and honor their right to do so. ". . . by abstaining from the possessions of others, we cannot better consult both these interests, than by such a convention (justice); because it is by that means we maintain society, which is so necessary to their well-being and subsistence, as well as to our own."[20] Appreciating the rights of others to earn and attain property while expecting the reciprocal appreciation for our rights to earn and retain that which is our own forms the fabric of a healthy society.

Alignment with Truth on Private Property Rights

Hume offers a perceived Atheist's perspective on private property and justice. What does the Church have to say about this topic? In his pre-eminent social Encyclical Letter, *Rerum Novarum*, Pope Leo XIII supports the rights of each human person to own his or her property. "Every man has by nature the right to possess property as his own."[21] When a laborer hires out to another his strength or his industry, he intends to acquire a full and real right, not only to the remuneration, but also to the disposal of that remuneration as he pleases. It is precisely in this power of disposal that ownership consists, whether the property be land or movable goods."[22] We all have a natural right to earn, attain, and acquire that which makes life possible and fulfilling.

Pope Leo establishes a working principle here. He wishes to show that the principle of private ownership is rooted in the law of nature or natural law, is in conformity with human nature, is enforced by legitimate civil law, and the authority of Divine Law.[23] He reiterates, "With reason, therefore, the common opinion of mankind, little affected by the few dissidents who have maintained the opposite view, has found in the study of nature, and in the law of nature herself, foundations of the division of property, and has consecrated by the practice of all ages the principle of private ownership, as being pre-eminently in conformity with human nature, and as conducing in the most unmistakable manner to the peace and tranquility of human life.[24] Do you see the similarity between Hume's emphasis on private property rights in the context of justice, and the Church's? Here faith and reason interface.

To ignore or abuse private property rights is condemned. Pope Leo continues, "The same principle is confirmed and enforced by the civil laws – laws which, as long as they are just, derive their binding force from the law of nature. The authority of the Divine Law adds its sanction, forbidding us in the gravest terms even to covet that which is another's: [Original Rerum Novarum text changed to Deuteronomy 5:21 (RSV) text for proper citation.] "Neither shall you covet your neighbor's wife; and you shall not desire your neighbor's house, his field, or his manservant, or his maidservant, his ox, or his ass, or anything that is your neighbor's."[25] Again, faith meets reason.

Summarily, inequality exists in nature. Man's universal and natural right to own that which he has justly earned renders inequality in what is earned simply because of differences in birthplace, birth homes, God-given skills, capacities, and learned capabilities, among other variables. This inequality gives rise to the need for the virtue of justice and the passive vice of injustice. As previously stated, the exercise of justice, from Hume's more narrow view, is a key to maintaining the fabric of society.

> **Unfortunately, Hume's view of justice falls short of the cardinal virtue of justice espoused by the Church.**

As we dive into Adam Smith's theories on morality, Smith leaned on Hume's truths. Like Hume, Smith rejects the argument that it is our benevolence or compassion that causes us to recoil from selfishly putting our own minor suffering ahead of the despair of millions. Smith states, "It is not the soft power of humanity, it is not the feeble spark of benevolence which Nature has lighted up in the human heart, that is thus capable of counteracting the strongest impulses of self-love."[26] Yet, from a Christian perspective, how much more is this spark of benevolence a raging fire if perfected and fanned by the flames of Christian faith, hope, and love? We ask this rhetorically now, but not so later and provide evidence of the "more."

Smith's ideas are much aligned with Hume's on the concept of justice yet are more refined and cautionary of what causes us to pursue justice for our personal preference and comfort.

> **Greed, ambition, and vanity are how Smith characterizes the vices that push us toward dissatisfaction with what we already have. He calls these vices "extravagant passions," and he warns us of their power.**

"Some of those situations (our job, our income, our wealth), no doubt, deserve to be preferred to others: but none of them can deserve to be pursued with that passionate ardour which drives us to violate the rules either of prudence or of justice; or to corrupt the future tranquility of our minds, either by shame from the remembrance of our folly, or by remorse from the horror of our own injustice."[27] Isn't Smith suggesting here that there is a nature of man or consequence anticipated by man that throttles down any pursuit of savage and solitary self-interest?

I suggest this question: Did Smith anticipate that the "horror of our own injustice" (looking in the mirror and knowing we have done wrong – hinting at a universal truth of "right") would come to pass due to these extravagant passions? I repeat, while Smith did not see us (you and me) as saints, he saw us clearly.[28]

Adam Smith's Observations on Virtue and Morality

Though known for his free market economic theory, fewer know Adam Smith was a Scottish moral philosopher. Before forming and writing about his economic theories, Smith sought to explain where morality comes from and why people can act with decency and virtue even when it conflicts with their own self-interest.[29] Smith believed that human beings are born as amoral beings, void of any morality except for the notion that we are the center of the universe. We cry, scream, wet, and soil as part of our natural biology and in pursuit of what we want. His philosophical premise is that we learn and grow through our exchanges and interactions with others; often judged by what Smith refers to as the "impartial spectator." This spectator may be our conscience, God, or some other imagined independent observer.

As toddlers, we learn that if we want to have a relationship with another human being, the amoral perspective with which we are born does not serve us well. Foraging for our own, not sharing, and hoarding what we have does not lend itself to healthy social relationships. (Reflect on Hume's description of this as 'savage and solitary' earlier in this chapter.) Smith comments, "If he would act so as that the impartial spectator (someone other than ourselves) may enter into the principle of his conduct . . . humble arrogance of his self-love, and bring it down to something which other men can go along with."[30] Our basic desire for social relationships and to belong; or as Smith puts it, to be loved and be lovely (worthy of love); tempers our self-center-of-the-universe sentiment. We begin to adjust our behavior to this changing reality. The other amoral toddler in our presence does the same, and so begins this dance of passions and sentiments.

> **Naturally, we begin to shed our self-centeredness out of concern for the other human being with whom we want to exchange and interact, desiring and expecting reciprocity.**

Multiply this by thousands of interactions over a lifetime, and our morality begins to form around what Adam Smith eloquently defines and thoroughly illustrates as the desire for mutual sympathy in sentiments. This desire for mutual sympathy in sentiments leads us, influenced by the impartial spectator, to pursue that which is inert in its harm to others, if not mutually beneficial. Smith shares, ". . . the natural misrepresentation of self-love can be corrected only by the eye of this impartial spectator. It is he who shows us the propriety of generosity and the deformity of injustice; the propriety of resigning the greatest interests of our own, for the yet greater interest of others, and the deformity of doing the smallest injury to another, in order to obtain the greatest benefit to ourselves."[31] Is not the world ignorant of this idea of conscience when judging the efficacy of free markets? Or is the absence of this ghostly impartial spectator from the consciousness of those exchanging goods and services in a free market the core problem?

In his book, *The Theory of Moral Sentiments*, written more than a decade before *The Wealth of Nations* and revised thereafter, Smith states, "Man naturally desires, not only to be loved, but to be lovely."[32] He means that we want people to like us, respect us, and care about us. We want to be appreciated, desired, praised, and cherished. We want people to pay attention to us and take us seriously. We want them to want our presence, to enjoy our company.[33] "Nothing pleases us more than to observe in other men a fellow-feeling with all the emotions of our own breast."[34] Smith adds, "If, upon bringing the case home to our own breast, we find that the sentiments which it gives occasion to, coincide and tally with our own, we necessarily approve of them as proportioned and suitable to the objects, if otherwise, we necessarily disapprove of them as extravagant and out of proportion."[35] In other words, what we want from others is for them to appreciate, love, or hold deeply that which we hold deeply. Others desire the same from us. We measure our approval of another's sentiment against the library of our own sentiments. Smith contends that propriety, the minimum standard for being "lovely," is about matching our responses to those around us.[36] The closer our sentiments match, the "lovelier" we are to our actual spectators. And we disapprove of sentiments that are incongruent with our own.

A modern way to capture what Smith is talking about when he talks about being loved and being lovely is authenticity. We want to be real, and we want the people around us to be real in how they think about us.

> "Respect or love or attention that is inaccurate because I don't deserve it isn't real."[37] – Dr. Brene Brown

Brene Brown, modern author of *Braving the Wilderness* and *Dare to Lead*, talks about being real as true belonging, and as respect, love, or attention that is inaccurate as just fitting in; a poor substitute for being yourself whether alone or in a crowd.[38] Her modern grounded theory research into true belonging and vulnerability validates many of Smith's inclinations.

In *The Theory of Moral Sentiments*, Smith reveals forces that work against the impartial spectator that serve to distort our sympathy in sentiments, and ultimately, our sense of morality. The first of these forces is our tendency toward self-deceit. We are prone to self-deception – the counsel we hear isn't quite as impartial as we would like to think. The imagined impartial spectator is an imperfect spokesperson for doing the right thing. Our urges (or passions) can easily overwhelm our judgment.[39] "It is so disagreeable to think ill of ourselves, that we often purposely turn away our view from those circumstances which might render that judgment unfavourable." Rather than see ourselves as we truly are, we see ourselves as we would like to be.[40] He continues, "This self-deceit, this fatal weakness of mankind, is the source of half the disorders of human life. If we saw ourselves in the light in which others see us, or in which they would see us if they know all, a reformation would generally be unavoidable. We could not otherwise endure the sight."[41] Self-deceit is a powerful force that pollutes our morality and the imagined objectivity of the impartial spectator who attempts to help us temper our self-interest.

The hubris and narcissism easily observable in many business leaders today is the modern manifestation of this self-deceit. Examining our conscience is the equivalent of attempting to mitigate this tendency toward self-deceit. Without a countervailing force like that of the Christian faith, Smith accurately predicts the outcome.

Another force working against the objectivity of the impartial spectator is the weight and honor given to people of wealth and power. Smith notes that the world pays attention to rich and famous and powerful people and not only to wise and virtuous people.

> ". . . upon coming into the world, we soon find that wisdom and virtue are by no means the sole objects of respect; nor vice and folly of contempt. We frequently see the respectful attentions of the world more strongly directed towards the rich and great, than towards the wise and the vituous."[42]

Something inside us reveres those who are revered. We idolize those who are idolized. We love those who are loved.[43] According to Smith, in the eyes of the rich and famous and powerful, all that attention appears to compensate them for all the drawbacks of getting to where they are and staying there.[44] Though the road of ambition is littered with proverbial corpses and carcasses of injustice, for the rich the ends often justify the means.

> **For Smith, ambition – the desire to be rich and famous or both – is a poison to be avoided.**

Where is this admonition considered in the understanding of Smith's free market theories or, more importantly, in the hearts and minds of those championing free markets? We certainly can see the truth of this poison in business today.

Despite his cautions about ambition, Smith is clear why we naturally choose to pursue wealth and fame. "It is because mankind is disposed to sympathize more entirely with our joy than with our sorrow, that we make parade of our riches, and conceal our poverty. Nothing is so mortifying as to be obliged to expose our distress to the view of the public, and to feel, that though our situation is open to the eyes of all mankind, no mortal conceives for us the half of what we suffer. Nay, it is chiefly from this regard to the sentiments of mankind, that we pursue riches and avoid poverty."[45] This honest insight hints at man's fundamental desire for dignity and informs and nudges the conscience of all of us who fear the stain of the condition of poverty. If you have ever been in a situation where you had to go to school wearing the dirty clothes you wore yesterday, you understand Smith's logic here. We do whatever we can to conceal our poverty and the related shame, and seek riches and provision to change this outcome.

Here is an essential summary offered by Smith, "And hence it is, that to feel much for others and little for ourselves, that to restrain our selfish, and indulge our benevolent affections, constitutes the perfection of human nature; and can alone produce among mankind that harmony of sentiments and passions in which consists their whole grace and propriety. As to love our neighbor as we love ourselves is the great law of Christianity, so it is the great precept of nature to love ourselves only as we love our neighbor, or what comes to the same thing, as our neighbor is capable of loving us."[46] Smith is right on with both our natural self-interest and our natural concern for others, but he bases our concern for others strictly on the affinity of one another's passions or sentiments; even placing our morals and sentiments in the hands of our imperfect neighbor and restricting our imperfect selves to a moral responsibility to "only as we love our neighbor;" or worse yet, "as much as our neighbor is capable of loving us."

This is not an exceedingly high bar without another influence, and certainly an unstable moral foundation given our tendency toward self-deception and skewed love for the rich, famous, and powerful.

Smith makes this statement that reveals his basis for determining actions to be considered moral. "When we judge in this manner of any affection, as proportioned or disproportioned to the cause which excites it, it is scarce possible that we should make use of any other rule or canon but the correspondent affection in ourselves."[47]

> **No need for any other "rule or canon" leaves morality to be determined by ourselves and the extent to which our sentiments dance with and agree to the sentiments of others.**

Do you see the lack of a moral keel here?! Certainly, without the regimen, if not the heart-felt compassion and mercy for the world emboldened and embodied by the Christian faith and the Church, we would find it scarcely possible to make use of any other set of rules for determining the appropriateness of another's actions as suggested by Adam Smith. With all due respect, I contend that herein lies Smith's folly.

Let's bring this discussion of Smith's morality and virtue home to free market economics and business; the topic for which Smith is most well-known. There is almost nothing about altruism or kindness or compassion or serenity or loveliness in *The Wealth of Nations*. Similarly, there is almost no defense of commercial life in *The Theory of Moral Sentiments*. Smith does concede in the latter, though, that great benefits for others can result – ambition induces us to strive, to innovate, to improve, to accumulate, to produce. In Smith's view, while we greatly exaggerate the benefits of accumulating wealth for our own happiness, ambition is what created agriculture; it made human beings create cities, and led us to discover the great truths of science and the arts and to "embellish human life."[48] "When Providence divided the earth among a few lordly masters, it neither forgot nor abandoned those who seem to have been left out in the partition. These last, too, enjoy their share of all that it produces."[49]

> Smith believes that the consequence of capital deployed in the interest of ascending to wealth and fame, though a vain and empty pursuit, benefits those within its wake; namely employees, laborers, trading partners, and society itself. This is a prophetic reference to trickle-down economic theory.

The modern calculus of economics, though, that looks at quantified benefits and costs only, is a flawed calculus.[50] I believe Adam Smith would be offended that today's economic man would ignore the cautions and insights provided in *The Theory of Moral Sentiments*. In many ways, his cautions were a harbinger of what we see today in business: an unhealthy worship of the rich and famous, an unbridled pursuit to mimic and achieve that lifestyle, and business actions passively endorsed by an amorphous morality that is defined by the masses who own and occupy the cultural megaphones. This amorphous morality in lieu of a fixed set of moral rules is Smith's folly.

Though a proponent of free markets and economic freedom generally, Smith was not an anarchist or a doctrinaire libertarian. He was a classical liberal, meaning a liberal in the original use of the word – someone who valued liberty and favored limited government. It is unlikely he could have foreseen the denigration of cultural norms to the point where tolerance is the great religion of modern times. Today, we all bow to it in ways that Smith would have found surprising.[51] "Shocking" may be a more appropriate descriptor here; adding unforeseen weight and color to his folly.

Chapter 1 Key Takeaways

1. Faith and reason support one another to reveal and affirm truth.

2. Hume's secular and rational perspective on justice and virtue informed Smith's ideologies.

3. Man has a natural right to earn, attain, and own private property.

4. Unequal magnitudes of owned private property are a prerequisite for the virtue of justice.

5. Concern for not violating the right of others to own private property gives rise to the secular virtue of justice.

6. Greed, ambition, and vanity are extravagant passions that Smith claims cause dissatisfaction with what we have.

7. We naturally begin to shed our self-centeredness over concern for those with whom we want a relationship or with whom we want to exchange. Smith calls this the desire for mutual sympathy in sentiments.

8. Smith's "impartial spectator" is the force that governs the propriety of our generosity and makes us aware of the deformity of our own injustice. No conscious "spectator;" no governor or voice of deformity.

9. Self-deceit impairs our ability to clearly judge others' sentiments. Another way to put this is we tend to judge others by their results or the outward manifestations of their sentiments, but we tend to judge ourselves by our intentions regardless of our outwardly manifested sentiments or results.

10. The rich and wealthy are equally as likely objects of our admiration and respect, as are wisdom and virtue.

11. Smith cautions us to avoid the poison of ambition – the desire to be rich and/or famous.

12. We love those who are "lovely" or rich and famous in a vain attempt to conceal our own poverty.

13. Other than sentiments, Smith contends there are no other canons or laws required to determine moral laws.

14. Absent other canons or laws, our morality is left married to the sentiments of others; wholly untethered to any fixed set of moral laws. I contend, herein lies Smith's folly.

Chapter 1 Synopsis

Those practicing and leading business in a free market ignorant of Adam Smith's moral philosophies and cautions are likely and unknowingly contributing to many of the abuses and perversions in business that we see today. Use both faith and reason to triangulate truth. The Chancellor at Baylor University shared this, "Faith does not compete with intellect. Faith completes it." Faith and reason support one another through the observance and experience of God's creation and natural law.

CHAPTER 2

The Impact of Adam Smith's Folly Today

ஒஓஒ

ADAM SMITH'S REPORTING OF morality formed by human beings disconnected from God and morphing without a tether to lasting human truths has had a profound impact on the world today. This is especially true in business. The ultimate question for us to answer is, "Can a free market function well without this moral tether?"

Where morality is ever-changing, as Smith suggests, moral truth is all but invisible. Most Christ-followers are very conscious of both the term and the manifestation of relative morality in today's world. Relativism is the idea that there is no universal, absolute truth but that truth differs from person to person, and culture to culture. In other words, truth is relative to what each person or culture thinks.[52] If truth does not exist, then, what I say goes for truth as does anyone else's say. Today, relativism is considered necessary to preserve peace and equality in our diverse world. You can see this assertion today when someone claims that he can know the truth with certainty about a religious or ethical issue (deeming himself a 'realist' vs. 'relativist'), he is usually labeled as intolerant, rigid, or closed-minded[53] - to use only kind words.

Today, what one says is informed most often by the greater culture or the megaphones manned by social media, the news media, talk show hosts, and others who offer logical and convincing arguments. In this way, the truth gets 'bent' out of shape, often to the point of clouding objective truth from sight. How much more is truth whitewashed when subjected to the approval and disapproval of others based simply on our selfish desire to be acknowledged and admired as Adam Smith suggests?

> Pope Emeritus Benedict XVI said, "... relativism, which recognizes nothing as definitive, leaves as the ultimate criterion only the self with its desires."[54]

This is wholly consistent with Smith's observations and frameworks for moral sentiments and the related consequences.

Tolerance is the one virtue a relativist society seems to value, but those who claim 'tolerance' likely don't understand its true meaning and context. To 'tolerate' something, you must first disagree with it! Tolerance, by definition, is enduring ideas or actions that you don't agree with.[55] One can still believe in objective truth and tolerate contrary beliefs. But one cannot not believe in objective truth and tolerate those who, too, do not believe in objective truth. Likewise, I cannot tolerate an inappropriate behavior in a circumstance if I condone or consider the behavior appropriate. That makes no sense. Tolerance is truly the religion of modern times, and Smith's amorphous morality is a contributor in the context of business. This fluctuating morality gives rise to this relevant and profound question, "What are you willing to give up in order to be 'lovely' (in this relativistic and tolerant world)?"[56] Remember, "lovely" is the term Adam Smith uses to describe those with whom we find congruence in sentiments. Brene Brown would argue that you become a stranger to yourself when you choose to fit in or be "lovely" vs. belong. True belonging demands that you be yourself; who God made you; and not abandon the essential you.[57] One of our biggest fears as human beings created to live in community is not belonging. So, we tend to go along with others who define "what is" and only change course if the greater culture leads us in that direction. We are the proverbial puppets guided by the greater-culture puppeteer.

Clouded Truth and Institutions

Another element that makes truth hard to see is what I will refer to as institutions. When I use the term, I am not talking about something venerable or long-lasting, though many are. I am using the term to describe a man-made practice or ideology to bring process and ease to something that is difficult. By the way, Smith understood well the human desire to make life easier, better, and faster.[58] We can use the institution of marriage as an example. The truth of marriage is hard; a man will leave his father and mother and marry a woman, becoming one. If you have been married, you know how hard it is to become one. To walk in lockstep with another through the world requires subordinating your interests for those of another. It is not always what you want for dinner or what you want to do. It's about what your spouse wants. This includes having children, moving to different places, working, and so much more! What the world sees today in marriage is almost 50% of marriages ending in divorce.[59] What they also see is an increasing number of unwed mothers, the ability to get married at a drive-through chapel in Las Vegas, and a $69 budget divorce kit. This is the institution of marriage that only vaguely mirrors the truth of marriage. The institution of marriage has become more about convenience than commitment.

Other institutions exist, too. Government is one of those. The institution of government is more about politics than principle. The diminishing guiding principles led by our nation's founding fathers have been subordinated to political posturing for purposes of reelection, preservation of status, and personal wealth and equity-building by many elected officials. Yet the truth of government still exists and it's about principle, not politics. Governing is hard! Let it be hard.

The truth of business, which is about purpose rather than profit, has been equally clouded by an institution. We will talk more about the dominant ideology later, but the institution of business is about maximizing shareholder wealth.

> **"Profit is the purpose for business" is no truer than oxygen is the purpose of life, yet oxygen is necessary for life.**

Likewise, profit is necessary for business life and that is where the Church hangs its hat. The Church acknowledges the legitimate role of profit as an indicator that a business is functioning well. When a firm makes a profit, it generally means that the factors of production have been properly employed and corresponding human needs have been duly satisfied.[60] A profitable business, by creating wealth, and promoting prosperity, helps individuals excel and realize the common good of a society.[61]

> **Between Smith's stated no need for any other "rule or canon" manifested as relative morality today and the man-made institutions built to add process and ease to something that is inherently difficult, we have a toxic cocktail of direction and speed with no moral keel.**

Free markets and business leaders without a moral "keel" or fixed set of rules lack that which allows them to function for the good of all mankind and the common good. We should state that there is substantial agreement in free market circles that protecting the right to own private property and the rule of law are also essential to the right and proper function of free markets. If we think of a well-functioning free market as the over-used illustration of a three-legged stool (I'm sorry for that, but will continue with it nevertheless), then I would argue that a fixed set of moral rules would be the third leg with private property rights and the rule of law the other two. Let's see if this thinking holds up under scrutiny.

Robert Heilbroner in his book, *The Essential Adam Smith,* states this about Smith's third theme of his moral sentiments which relates to the problem of morality:

> "A socially stable society is a prerequisite for an economically successful one."[62]

He asks the reader, "How can human beings, who are presumably captives to their own self-interest, suspend selfish considerations to form disinterested 'moral' judgments?[63] Smith surprisingly gives some insight in the opening sentence of his *Theory of Moral Sentiments.* "How selfish so ever man may be supposed, there are evidently some principles in his nature, which interest him in the fortune of others, and render their happiness necessary to him, though he derives nothing from it, except the pleasure of seeing it."[64]

What are these principles in his nature and from where do they emanate? Heilbroner goes on in his commentary to define Smith's "virtue" as the embodiment of morality. He adds, "It (morality) therefore is not reducible to a fixed set of rules. It is always mediated by the empathetic properties of human understanding. Morality is not given to us, but made by ourselves."[65] History, again, informs us that this type of thinking aligns well with the period known as the Enlightenment, supposedly freeing man from the bonds and restrictive principles of right and wrong by any fixed moral code presupposed and taught by the Church. Today, this has led us now to a moral code that allows for gender to be a human choice, life in the womb to be subject to a mother's preference and convenience, and marriage to be about equality of rights versus God-designed procreation, among many other allowances thought only a decade ago to be sacrosanct!

If a "socially stable society" is a prerequisite for an economically successful one, then is it reasonable to doubt that "morality made by ourselves" can produce such a society? Smith argues, though, that to have societal harmony, "There will never be unisons, there may be concords, and this is all that is wanted or required."[66] Yet today our society in the U.S. is arguably as unstable as it has been since the debates and battles over slavery more than a century ago.

> **A culture that was once dominated by church-going and God-fearing Christians is now dominated by those who practice morality of one's own making.**

This has resulted in a moral line that has shifted, and any attempt to speak the truth relegates the speaker to one of two options: conform to what is or be expelled to the fringes of society. Christians are being expelled in droves to the fringes of the culture in this post-truth society. As evidence, the over-used label of 'phobia' or 'phobic' - a type of overwhelming or debilitating fear of an object, place, situation, feeling or animal - is attached to anything today that resembles truth. If you choose to disagree with a homosexual lifestyle, even respectfully, you are deemed homophobic. If you are transparent and verbalize discomfort, respectfully, with those of other ethnicities, you are branded xenophobic. What is being expressed is simply a disagreement or discomfort, not a debilitating fear, yet the misunderstood concept of tolerance today rules.

Where has this "morality made by ourselves" left us in business? As odd as this may sound, Adam Smith, himself, gave us some insight.

> "This disposition to admire, and almost to worship the rich and the powerful, and to despise, or, at least, to neglect persons of poor and mean condition . . . is the great and most universal cause of the corruption of our moral sentiments."[67]

There is an experienced and observable difference between the admiration we offer the rich and successful versus the poor and meek, is there not? How many of us desire to change places with the impoverished yet would jump at the chance to trade places with the rich? Smith puts it this way, "Our obsequiousness (flattery) to our superiors more frequently arises from our admiration for the advantages of their situation, than from any private expectations of benefit from their goodwill."[68] Remember the famous quotation shared earlier from Smith's *Wealth of Nations*? "It is not from the benevolence of the butcher, the brewer, or the baker that we expect our dinner, but from their regard to their own self-interest."[69] Therein manifests this idea.

This, what I would call "idolatry" of the rich, has led businesspeople to seek that which enriches themselves, reinforced by the dominant ideology - the purpose of business is to maximize shareholder wealth. Those who aren't shareholders easily extrapolate this ideology to themselves and their individual pursuit of something more. Everyone feels free to be in business, figuratively, for themselves. This is not an indictment of mature ambition, nor to desire more and better for yourself and family. This is the benefit of self-interest! We all want this and free markets can deliver it. But absent the third leg of the three-legged free market stool – a fixed set of moral rules – this desire for more and the lack of concern for the poor and meek, much less that which benefits the common good, leaves our society with the following:

- a concentration of wealth in a few,
- excessive and exorbitant executive compensation justified by comparative equity across industry executives with little regard for equity or contribution inside the business enterprise,
- many non-owners whose economic stake is essentially fixed or declining,
- an abdication of responsibility to the State to care for those marginalized in society,
- and a polarizing of society between those who-have and those who have-not.

Smith offers the following as an antidote for immature ambition; the need to ascend to a place of power and wealth, for the sole sake of power and wealth: "Never enter the place from whence so few have been able to return; never come within the circle of ambition; nor ever bring yourself into comparison with those masters of the earth who have already engrossed the attention of half mankind before you."[70] He summarizes this thought by quoting Lord Rochefoucauld:

> "Love is commonly succeeded (followed) by ambition, but ambition is hardly ever succeeded (followed) by love."[71]

Likewise, if God is love, then God must precede ambition. But if this truth is denied, then individual ambition has and will have its way with and throughout business. This harsh pursuit of personal ambition, often to the detriment of others, is certainly visible in business today and Smith cautioned of its underow.

I'm fond of saying that death is the great equalizer – something inescapable by every human person that forces the bequeathing of one's accumulated property to the hands of others. Similarly, Smith acknowledged one of the most important principles in human nature in his book *The Theory of Moral Sentiments*, ". . . the dread of death, the great poison to the happiness, but the great restraint upon the injustice of mankind, which, while it afflicts and mortifies the individual, guards and protects the society."[72] His argument is that the fear of death is a strong motivator for justice and, as such, helps man govern and stabilize society.

> **I can't help but wonder how the length and luxury of life today makes any fear of death less a motivator for justice than in the 18th Century when he wrote his books.**

Regardless, as Christians we are reminded in the Bible from Matthew 10:39 (NIV), "Whoever finds his life will lose it, and whoever loses his life for my sake will find it."[73] Our lives on this earth are temporary. Our intended eternal dwelling place is with God in heaven, and this should inform our work, our business, our ambition, and our moral standards.

The Deadly Sins of Pride and Envy

Sin is an invited guest in a free market economy absent truth. In the Introduction, I spoke of the more sinister side of pride. Those of us who 'have' are justifiably proud of our accomplishments, though some would argue that those with privilege haven't "hit a home run;" we have just been blessed to start at third base. Envy, the more sinister side of pride, causes one to covet possessions of another. Envy is one of seven deadly sins, along with pride, greed, lust, gluttony, anger, and sloth.[74]

> **Pride is a self-imposed deadly sin, and its subtle intention is to create envy in others. Envy, as a targeted consequence of pride, is a sin to which others are drawn.**

Matthew 5:19 (NIV) reminds us, "Anyone who breaks one of the least of these commandments and teaches others to do the same will be called least in the kingdom of heaven."[75] Without temperance as a guiding moral virtue, the excessive materialism that grips so many often draws those who have-not into the sin of envy.

> **Consider this hard truth - when we in business hold out our accomplishments and our possessions in ways that draw attention to ourselves, we are literally drawing others into the deadly sin of envy.**

We often do this without aforethought in today's world by driving vehicles that speak to status versus value and functionality.

We over-extend ourselves through debt and readily available credit facilities, both personally and in business. We masquerade as having our homes and relationships together when inside the walls of our houses everything is falling apart. We judge our children by the amount of pride they generate for us so we can produce envy from others. For that we will eventually answer to our Creator.

Adam Smith addressed envy in this way, "The man who, by some sudden revolution of fortune, is lifted up all at once into a condition of life, greatly above what he had formerly lived in, may be assured that the congratulations of his best friends are not all of the perfectly sincere."[76] Jealousy and envy look similar on the surface, but jealousy is a rational response to gains of others earned. Envy is a response to gains of others ill-earned or perceived as not deserved. The difference between jealousy and envy is a thin line.

> **The risk of being perceived as achieving success at the expense of others versus with and for others has significant implications on our journey and the way we choose to do business.**

Must the Poor be Excluded from Free Markets

Let's take a deeper look at the effect of free markets on the poor. I will suggest to you that 'the poor' is not a class of people you can point to, but a condition that any human being can find him or herself in at any particular time. The condition of poverty is often manifested in a corresponding insecurity and these insecurities can be uniquely defined.

For instance, food insecurity is the condition of not knowing from where your next meal will come. Any of us could be in this situation at any given time. I would argue that this insecurity places us in the condition of poverty. The Bible speaks clearly about the poor in spirit inheriting the earth. Why? Because people suffering insecurity must rely on their faith for provision – a need for which those of us who-have were made to fulfill in ways that not only aid others but promote the dignity of those in that condition.

> **Those of us who-have do not need faith for our provision, so we can often become complacent in our faith and complicit in our ignorance of those in the condition of poverty, chalking up their condition to a consequence of action or inaction by the subject in poverty.**

We eat more than we ought without regard for others who are hungry; we spend more than we ought ignorant of alternative and better uses for our monies; we consume without thanksgiving and praise to our Creator as if we have authored every step of our journey.

Another example is shelter insecurity. This is a condition where one does not know where he or she will lay their head down at night (i.e., homelessness). Again, any of us could find ourselves in this condition. When we have shelter or a home, we are expected to provide for those who have not. Yes, this expectation demands the use of our private property to be used for the benefit of another. In Catholic Social Teaching, this is the concept of the universal destination of goods. While the Church is absolute in its support for the inalienable right to private ownership of property as previously shared, the ownership of private property is always subordinated to the universal destination of goods – the idea that God made available goods to be owned privately, yet to be used for the benefit of not just the owner, but for those within the care of and community of those with private property.

How many unused bedrooms or bathrooms are in your house? Do you have the financial wherewithal to purchase a home, make the monthly payments and help a homeless family solve their shelter insecurity problem? Have you considered adopting or fostering orphans? These are probing and sharp questions for those of us who find comfort in our success.

This is hard Church teaching. This may involve giving away or making available personal assets such as vehicles or rooms in your home, but it's more the manifestation of the virtues of justice and temperance in individual persons for the purpose of charity or love of one's neighbor – the second element of the great commandment. Absent this truth, are we not left with materialism to the neglect of the most marginalized in our society?

Conditions of poverty other than food and shelter insecurity include the following:

- Transportation insecurity – how will I get from here to there – work, home, doctor, store?
- Job insecurity – will I be working to produce enough income for me and my family?
- Skill insecurity – are my skills satisfactory for gainful employment and progress consistent with my God-given capabilities?
- Education insecurity – are my primary reading, writing, math, and science skills satisfactory to support skills development and are they consistent with my God-given capabilities?
- Family insecurity – is my home a place that fosters an environment for academic achievement and for gender role modeling and maturity?

When the answer to any of these questions is "no," that insecurity is the manifestation of the condition of poverty. When we view poverty this way and understand it as a condition, not a class of people, we can avoid objectifying those in this condition and can begin to consider how those of us who-have, can help to create sustainable and transformational solutions for those who have-not.

The Church expects its followers to have a preference for those in the condition of poverty. Saint John Paul II used the word "solidarity" to describe a person's chosen commitment to the good of others as a specific moral attitude and virtue. It cannot therefore be mistaken for vague sentimentalism. It is a 'firm and persevering determination' to commit oneself to the common good; that is to say to the good of all and each individual, because we are all really responsible for all.[77]

Michael Matheson Miller of the Acton Institute, in his Sustainable and Transformational (SAT Talks - October 2015) presentation entitled *Charity 1.0* clarified that charity or love disjoined from truth is the same sentimentality referred to by Saint John Paul II above. It's a hollowed-out version of charity that is shallow in depth and materialistic in its primary benefit. He goes further to name this shallow sentimentalism as humanitarianism.[78]

This is not the charity of which God speaks. Humanitarianism can easily become the State helping your neighbor versus you helping your neighbor. It can also evolve into what Tom Bassford with Significant Matters calls "benevolent narcissism" or giving to philanthropies or causes to make ourselves feel better. We write checks which are very good and used for good, but they fall short of the integrated human experience expected between you and your neighbor. We abdicate that responsibility when hollow humanitarianism becomes the manifestation of our charity.

As a virtue, solidarity needs to become as much a moral habit as something like courage or temperance.[79] Virtues, moreover, are only realized when a person freely commits himself to acting consistently for the good. This is why Saint John Paul II stressed that "an essential condition" for living out the virtue of solidarity "is autonomy and free self-determination."[80] This essential autonomy is intuitively part of an unrestricted, unrestrained free market economy and laissez-faire government. The only question is, will we choose it. I repeat, the Church has long taught that the value of any economic system rests on the personal virtue of the individuals who take part in it.[81]

How do we build a concern for liberty and human flourishing into the way that all institutions and communities help to promote solidarity in a given society, especially in business?[82]

> Solidarity finds its ultimate end not in some earthly
> Rousseauian utopia of universal brotherhood, but
> rather in promoting the conditions that facilitate
> human flourishing.[83] – Samuel Gregg

Business leaders are uniquely positioned and God-ordained (as a vocation) to contribute to the conditions and environment that allow people to flourish. How much different is this calling or purpose from that of maximizing profit? Yet, as we will logically prove in this book, when you allow people to flourish and cooperate fully at work, your business will be better than had you not.

How do free markets, businesses operating therein, and business leaders absent truth meet this standard of charity, solidarity, and human flourishing? If the agreeable moral standard or sentiment is now the shallow and materialistic humanitarianism, I would suggest not well. That is not to say that there are not generous and caring businesses with generous and caring business leaders, but how much more could be done if the truth was catalytic in a transcendent business? You'll find examples of virtuous business leaders and transcendent businesses in the section of this book entitled Virtuosos.

We've practiced free market capitalism ignorant of Adam Smith's cautions because we simply didn't know. Now we do. We have allowed our moral keel to shift by willingly accepting Adam Smith's free market and laissez-faire government aspirations, while blindly allowing his amorphous moral presuppositions to ride along much like a parasite covertly imbeds in a host. The teachings of the Church were long lost in the age of Enlightenment, yet they speak of many of the same principles that caused Adam Smith pause as he pondered the ultimate outcome of a hopelessly selfish man.

If free market capitalism is to continue its potential beneficence for all, regardless of its pace, then those practicing capitalism must reacquaint themselves with the cautions contemplated by Adam Smith and embrace the virtues espoused by the Church.

The free market economy in the U.S., absent the third leg of the free market stool – a fixed set of moral rules – is now generating a response seen previously in world history. We see the heightened interest in and specter of socialism on the horizon. I argue that socialism is a lagging indicator of injustice. This is not surprising given the man-made, do-no-harm sense of justice of which Hume and Adam Smith speak native to a free market moral philosophy absent a fixed set of moral principles or the truth. The virtue of justice of which the Church speaks is that which is much higher still; that which is due each human being simply because they are created in the image of God. This is to what businesses and Christian business leaders must ascend. The economic idea of socialism is gaining momentum in our society and it is antithetical to liberty, human flourishing, and truth, and, as the next Chapter demonstrates, the Church pulls no punches in condemning it.

Chapter 2 Key Takeaways

1. Relativism, which recognizes nothing as definitive, leaves as the ultimate criterion for morality only the self with its desires, consistent with Smith's philosophies.
2. Are you willing to sell your soul to be "lovely" or fit in, much like Esau traded his birthright for a bowl of soup?
3. Institutions are man-made creations that mask hard teachings and only vaguely mirror the truth.
4. The combination of no other rule or canon other than sentiments and the impact of institutions is a toxic cocktail offering businesses speed and direction with no moral keel.
5. A well-functioning free market requires three elements:
    a. The right to private property
    b. The rule of law
    c. A fixed set of moral rules
6. A socially stable society is a prerequisite for an economically successful society.

7. Amorphous morality "made by ourselves" post-Enlightenment creates societal instability and any hint of truth-telling relegates one to the fringes of society.

8. The disposition to admire and worship the rich and famous and not concern ourselves with those who are not, is the great and universal cause of the corruption of our moral sentiments.

9. This worship of the rich and famous, coupled with the dominant ideology regarding the purpose of business invites business leaders to pursue wealth at the expense of others versus with and through others.

10. Since love precedes ambition and rarely vice versa, God must precede ambition.

11. Poverty is not a person or people group. It's a condition in which any of us can find ourselves. In a free market, there are ways to move out of poverty and protect the human dignity of those in the condition of poverty.

12. Pride is an imposed sin. The real danger is its counterpart – envy. Envy is what those with pride generate or seek from others, drawing them into sin. For this we will have to answer.

13. Solidarity with the poor forces us to redefine charity and the purpose of business.

14. Businesses are intended to, and business leaders are gifted to create the conditions for human flourishing, if business leaders would only ascend to that role and purpose.

15. Socialism, a lagging indicator of injustice, is a rising response to the social instability evidenced today.

Chapter 2 Synopsis

The idea of an amorphous or ever-changing morality is at the heart of an ill-functioning free market, capitalist system. A well-functioning free market must have a fixed set of moral rules, manifested through virtue practiced by those participating in business. Anything short of that yields charity that is secular humanitarianism and the ill-functioning market and related inequity triggers a response, socialism; a lagging indicator of injustice.

CHAPTER 3

Socialism's Flaws

∿⊙⊘∿

I DO NOT MINCE words here. "Folly" would be insufficient to describe the nature of socialism and its idealistic promise to those who pursue it. "Flaws" is more accurate. To those who pursue social justice, which we all should, socialism provides a false promise, but a promise, nevertheless. I would argue that hope of prosperity for all in a free market or capitalist economy has waned so much that those left in the margin; those enduring years of job and/or earnings stagnation or decline against the cost of living and living paycheck-to-paycheck; those now dependent on government assistance for their sustenance; and those watching enviously of others who are thriving and gaining wealth are left few options but to pursue a promise of anything other than "what is." As history has shown, sometimes this pursuit is revolutionary when the fever of the people peaks, and the real or perceived injustice is shared by a growing number of citizens.

The revolutionaries, though, ignorantly trade that which is most valuable for an imperfect promise and a less-perfect correction. Friedrich Hayek, in his book, *The Road to Serfdom*, states:

> "People don't intend to trade away their most basic
> freedoms. They just want more economic equality
> and more financial security."[84]

In today's culture and lexicon, the desire for more financial security is manifested in the concern over mounting tuition and related student debt post-graduation from college, as well as rising consumer and credit card debt, among other financial burdens common to many individuals and households. Millennials want relief from this burden, but they aren't necessarily interested in trading away their inherent freedoms. They just don't connect the dots.

When faced with the pallor of a capitalism without virtue, people are easily misled by a pseudo-ideal of justice, of equality, and of fraternity of labor. This is very compelling for those who have-not and who view those who have, with envy.[85] Recall our discussion that those in the condition of poverty are more exposed than others to the wiles of agitators who, taking advantage of their extreme need, kindle envy of the rich (one-of-seven deadly sins), and urge them to seize by force what fortune seems to have been denied them under the watchful eye of justice.[86] Leaders with socialist ideologies sharpen the antagonisms that arise between the different classes of society. This class struggle takes on the aspects of a crusade for the progress of humanity.[87] Ultimately, workers are recruited through trickery of various forms while the truth is clouded by ideals that in themselves are good and attractive; including that of social justice which is arguably the common ground toward which humanity in the economic sector should ascend.[88] This is happening now in the U.S. with the rise of Democratic Socialism as a political ideology and talk of "New Deal" programs that place the progress of humanity in the hands of government or the State.

Hayek on Socialism

The rise of socialism, though, while revolutionary in nature; an attempt to reorganize the entirety of society; is more like the proverbial frog in boiling water lesson. If you abruptly drop a frog in boiling water, he will immediately jump out. If you place a frog in water at ambient temperature and then bring it slowly to a boil, the frog will stay in the water. Hayek, the Nobel Prize-winning economist, would argue that the west has been in a centuries-long slow movement away from classic liberal economics, where liberty and freedom of citizens to act are inviolable rights.[89] Although we had been warned by some of the greatest political thinkers of the 19th Century; by Tocqueville and Lord Acton; that socialism means slavery, we have steadily moved in the direction of socialism.[90]

> Surprisingly, probably nothing has done so much harm to the liberal cause as the wooden insistence of some liberals (in economic not political terms) to certain rough rules of thumb, above all the principle of laissez-faire.[91] – Friedrich Hayek

In Libertarian political circles today, this stubborn attempt to minimize government is the modern equivalent of "wooden insistence" today. Notice that any discussion of the Church, of virtue, or of truth is absent in this conversation. While the other two legs of the effective free market stool; the right to private property and the rule of law receive their due endorsement from Libertarians, the rough rules of thumb, absent the sway of virtue and truth are dangerous precursors to socialism and slavery.

Progress in a liberal (free) society is necessarily slow. Hayek contends that the attitude of a liberal society is like that of a gardener who tends a plant and, in order to create the conditions most favorable to its growth, must know as much as possible about its structure and the way it functions.[92] While the progress toward what is commonly called "positive" action was necessarily slow, and while for the immediate improvement liberalism had to rely largely on the gradual increase of wealth which freedom brought about, it had constantly to fight proposals which threatened this progress.

> The slow progress came to be regarded as "negative" because it could offer to particular individuals little more than a share in the common progress – a progress which came to be taken more and more for granted and was no longer recognized as the result of the policy of freedom. It might even be said that the very success of liberalism became the cause of its decline.[93] – Friedrich Hayek

The rising tide of progress in a free market economy, while lifting all boats, has lost its mooring from the cause of freedom. Progress is simply a blind derivative of freedom, and unequal progress among individuals in a free market economy is the spark that continues to burn the slow wick toward socialism.

The complacency associated with taking progress for granted in a free market economy has contributed greatly to its dilution toward demise. What had been achieved (slow, though continual progress for many) came to be regarded as a secure and imperishable possession, acquired once and for all. The eyes of the people became fixed on the new demands, the rapid satisfaction of which seemed to be barred by the adherence to the old principles. It became more and more widely accepted that further advance could be expected not along old lines within the general framework (of liberalism) which had made past progress possible, but only by a complete remodeling of society (the elimination of private property and the control of the means of production by the government). And, as the hope of the new generation came to be centered on something completely new, interest in and understanding of the functioning of the existing society rapidly declined; and, with the decline of the understanding of the way in which the free system worked, our awareness of what depended on its existence also decreased.[94]

It is easy for me to empathize with those left in the margins subject to the slow growth in economic wealth for themselves, while others around them thrive. A very negative undertone can accompany this dissatisfaction especially if the gains accruing to others, are perceived as ill-gotten versus legitimately earned. It's this negative undertone accompanying the dissatisfaction that is attracting the attention of many who seek social justice; even while ignorantly giving up their freedom and liberty. This is all happening under the watchful gaze of justice; that which intends to give others what is due them simply because of their inherent dignity because they have been created in the image and likeness of God. Yet today justice must squint to see in the dark, absent the light of this truth.

While the term "democratic socialism" has found fertile soil in the modern U.S. political arena, its use dates back to the mid-19th century, when it struggled to live down the suspicions aroused by its antecedents.[95] Tocqueville, again, cautioned that Democracy is an essential individualist institution stood as an irreconcilable conflict with socialism. "Democracy extends the sphere of individual freedom," he said in 1848; "socialism restricts it. Democracy attaches all possible value to each man; socialism makes each man a mere agent, a mere number.

> Democracy and Socialism have nothing in common
> but one word: equality. But notice the difference:
> while Democracy seeks equality in liberty, Socialism
> seeks equality in restraint and servitude."[96] – Friedrich
> Hayek

Overcoming previous suspicions, the demand for the new freedom was thus only another name for the old demand for an equal distribution of wealth.[97] Democratic Socialism, the great utopia of the last few generations, is not only unachievable, but to strive for it produces something so utterly different that few of those who now wish it would be prepared to accept the consequences.[98] What is promised to us as the Road to Freedom is in fact the High Road to Servitude.[99]

Often, the concept of socialism is used to describe the ideals of social justice, greater equality, and security. But it also means the particular method or methods by which most socialists hope to attain these ends and which many competent people regard as the only methods by which they can be fully and quickly attained. In this sense, socialism means the abolition of private enterprise, of private ownership of the means of production, and the creation of a system of "planned economy" in which the entrepreneur working for profit is replaced by a central planning body.[100]

While obviously jaded toward the benefits and progress in a free market economy, Hayek refuses to throw out the baby with the bathwater. There are many people who call themselves Socialists, although they care only about the ideals of socialism; they fervently believe in those ultimate aims of socialism (social justice, greater equality, and security) but neither care nor understand how they can be achieved, and who are merely certain that they must be achieved, whatever the cost. Many people, on the other hand, who value the ultimate ends of socialism no less than the Socialists, refuse to support socialism because of the dangers to other values they see in the methods proposed by the Socialists.

> "The dispute about socialism has thus become a dispute about means and not about ends. Those who repudiate the means, value the ends."[101] – Friedrich Hayek

What is of ultimate concern here, is not socialism's moral basis, but its moral results.[102] Yet with no moral keel, how are those compelled by the false promise of socialism and, especially, those expecting to be part of the central planning elite, to judge socialism on its historically proven lack of merit?

The Church on Socialism

History has shown, that while the ends of socialism are admirable and the pursuit thereof worthy of our best effort, socialism is a flawed option. On the other hand, history has shown that capitalism produces both economic growth and real human flourishing, or at least the significant potential thereof. Yet without some form of moral keel, or fixed set of rules, capitalism can leave social justice wanting. "Without internal forms of solidarity and mutual trust, the (free) market cannot completely fulfill its proper economic function."[103] Pope Emeritus Benedict's prime interest here was in helping make the economy a realm in which the virtuous habits associated with love of neighbor can be exercised in conjunction with and alongside people's pursuit of self-interest.[104] Naturally, no amount of generosity makes-up for basic violations of justice.[105]

> **A free and virtuous society is the goal; not a dog-eat-dog world where only the strong survive, you eat only what you kill, and only those who attain wealth practice benevolence too often for their own perceived benefit.**

We will discuss what a business might look like if virtue was a part of its business equation and transcendence was its ultimate end in the next chapter, but let's first give socialism its due as an alternative to capitalism.

The Church has certainly given socialism significant attention over the last century-plus, just as it demands our attention and effort toward social justice; arguably the force behind the peoples' pursuit of something other than "what is." A healthy mind-set here is to honor those suffering injustices and wanting more for them; not to throw them out with the socialist ideology when its flaws are revealed. Injustices and suffering still exist that require our attention as Christian business leaders and as a Christian community. By no stretch of the imagination can the Church be regarded as opposed in principle to governments seeking to help those in need. But alongside these axioms, the Church has continually reminded Catholics that as individuals and as a religious community, they have concrete responsibilities to their neighbor which are not fulfilled by voting for expansive government welfare programs or even paying taxes that fund such activities.[106]

Today, there are no true communist countries in the world, but several countries who practice socialism in some form. I will use the terms communism and socialism interchangeably in this book. We will start this off with a blunt conclusion offered by the Church.

> "Socialism is intrinsically wrong, and no one desiring to further Christianity should collaborate with it in any way."[107] – PopePius XI

In this case, it can be said that the proposed cure is worse than the disease. Yes, a virtue-starved capitalism or free market can concentrate wealth and power in a few and leave large portions of society relegated to the margin, but this disease is far better than the moral consequences of socialism and the necessary restraint of liberty and freedom that accompany it.

> **Not only does socialism not address the root cause problem that gives rise to communist/socialist ideologies, but it diminishes, if not outlaws that which is an essential part of the solution; the ancient religion and its impact on the personal virtues of the individuals who take part in commerce and lead in business.**

The Church shares that socialism is by its nature anti-religious. Socialists consider religion an "opiate of the people," poisoning their minds with thoughts of life beyond the grave; dissuading the workers or proletariat from the dream of a more equal utopia on this earth.[108] The Church goes on to suggest, "The infamous doctrine of so-called communism which is absolutely contrary to the natural law itself, and if once adopted, would utterly destroy the rights, property, and possessions of all men, and even society itself."[109] The communist/socialist ideology holds out the promise of absolute equality, rejecting all hierarchy and divinely-constituted authority, including the authority of parents. Nor is the individual granted any property rights over material goods or the means of production in a Socialist State.[110] The contradiction of these tenets of socialism to the Church's insistence on the right to private ownership of property should not go unnoticed. When a religious institution becomes dependent on the state, political control eventually follows, and "He who drinks the King's wine sings the King's songs."[111] The voices of the people go silent, not from dissent, but from the heavy-handed response to any threat of usurping central economic authority.

Pope Leo XIII in his foundational Encyclical *Rerum Novarum*, clearly cautions us against the ills and evils of socialism, even while condemning the plight of the working man who is being subjected to harsh working conditions, the hard-heartedness of employers, and the greed of unchecked competition. "To remedy these wrongs the Socialists, working on the poor man's envy of the rich, are striving to do away with private property, and contend that individual possessions should become the common property of all, to be administered by the State or by municipal bodies. They hold that by thus transferring property from private individuals to the community, the present mischievous state of things will be set to rights, inasmuch as each citizen will then get his fair share of whatever there is to enjoy. But their contentions are so clearly powerless to end the controversy that were they carried into effect the working man himself would be among the first to suffer. They are, moreover, emphatically unjust, for they would rob the lawful possessor, distort the functions of the State, and create utter confusion in the community."[112]

Pope Leo continues, "And in addition to injustice, it is only too evident what an upset and disturbance there would be in all classes, and to how intolerable and hateful a slavery citizens would be subjected. The door would be thrown open to envy, to mutual invective, and to discord; the sources of wealth themselves would run dry, for no one would have any interest in exerting his talents or his industry; and that ideal equality about which they entertain pleasant dreams would be in reality the leveling down of all to a like condition of misery and degradation. Hence, it is clear that the main tenet of socialism, community of goods, **must be utterly rejected**, since it only injures those whom it would seem meant to benefit, is directly contrary to the natural rights of mankind, and would introduce confusion and disorder into the commonwealth. The first and most fundamental principle, therefore, if one would undertake to alleviate the condition of the masses, must be the inviolability of private property."[113] [Bold added for emphasis.] The Holy Bible records Jesus expressing, "But wisdom is proved right by her actions" (Matthew 11:19b NIV), when the truth of John the Baptist was questioned by others, as was Jesus' own identity. If you doubt what is suggested as the consequences of socialism, you need only to look at history's record thereof.

Pope Leo ends this section of his Encyclical with the promise of providing insight into what to do to address the core problem. The wisdom, not only of his insights into the flaws of socialism, but into the root cause problem and the elements of the solution are just as relevant today as they were in the 19th Century.

The Role the State is Not to Play

The government or State has a role to play in ensuring the protection of human dignity and the pursuit of the common good, but in the economic sector, the primary responsibility is not theirs. Many Catholics with a heart for the poor and under-resourced see the government as the answer. This is not what the Church teaches. The State is to act as a backstop and insurer only.

> ". . . primary responsibility in the area (overseeing and directing the exercise of human rights in the economic sector) belongs not to the State, but to individuals and to the various groups and associations which make up society."[114] – Saint John Paul II

This expectation is consistent with the Catholic Social Doctrine of subsidiarity. The principle of subsidiarity holds that a community of a higher order should not interfere in the internal life of a community of a lower order, depriving the latter of its function, but rather should support it in case of need and help to coordinate its activity with the activities of the rest of society, always with a view to the common good.[115] "Just as it is gravely wrong to take from individuals what they can accomplish by their own initiative and industry and give it to the community, so also it is an injustice and at the same time a grave evil and disturbance of right order to assign to a higher association what lesser and subordinate organizations can do. For every social action ought of its very nature furnish help to the members of the body social, and never destroy and absorb them."[116] The solution proposed by socialism, a wholesale re-ordering of society, is consequently in direct contrast to this teaching.

Experience shows that the denial of subsidiarity, or its limitation in the name of an alleged democratization or equality of all members of society, limits and sometimes even destroys the spirit of freedom and initiative. As Hayek suggests, people don't willingly trade away their freedom and liberty. They know only that the pace of their gains is outstripped by others within their purview; forgetting that that same freedom and liberty is what brought even the meager gains they've experienced. Once traded away, it could be argued given what we observe today in the most socialist-oriented countries of the world, that the real value of freedom and liberty is learned and any value of unearned equality promised by socialism pales in comparison.

The principle of subsidiarity is opposed to certain forms of centralization, bureaucratization, and welfare assistance and to the unjustified and excessive presence of the State in public mechanisms. There are times, though, where one could envision the need for the State to intervene as the insurer or guardian of the common good and the protector of human dignity, where perhaps a serious social imbalance or injustice exists. In light of the principle of subsidiarity, however, this institutional substitution must not continue any longer than is absolutely necessary, since justification for such intervention is found only in the exceptional nature of the situation.[117]

> **This Church teaching places a discount on State intervention, unlike the premium placed on the same by the principles of socialism and demands limited time and scope for intervention.**

How then is a neighbor, community, city, county, state, or country, absent a fixed set of moral rules and a true understanding and embodiment of virtue, to adjust and give the State confidence that the root cause problem is identified, fixed, and covered? This is especially relevant when the root cause problem is the setting aside of the ancient religion and all its precepts and teachings. Would not the State absent trust that the situation would improve remain involved longer and deeper? My intuition says it would and it does. I believe 20th Century government programs provide ample evidence of this.

In his Encyclical Letter, *Deus Caritas Est*, Pope Emeritus Benedict XVI writes, "Love, or *caritas*, will always prove necessary, even in the most just society. There is no ordering of the State so just that it can eliminate the need for the service of love. The State which would provide everything, absorbing everything into itself, would ultimately become . . . incapable of guaranteeing the very thing which . . . every person needs, namely loving, personal concern. We do not need a State which regulates and controls everything, but a State which, in accordance with the principle of subsidiarity, generously acknowledges and supports initiatives arising from the different social forces and combines spontaneity with closeness to those in need."[118]

The implications of the Catholic Social Principle of subsidiarity are profound on business, business leaders, and employees who profess belief in the tenets of the Church and acknowledge a belief in and follow Jesus Christ.

> **We have an absolute responsibility to nurture and love those entrusted to our care at work and those who live and work within our communities.**

Absent us taking the responsibility, we invite longer-than-desired State intervention as the insurer and guardian. These interventions become formal programs that, as we have seen, can breed dependence and a sense of entitlement from those benefiting. We can begin to see how the threat of socialism in our society has slowly evolved from two significant, uniquely-free-market forces: 1) the meager gains of many while they observe others' more significant gains; often observed to be ill-gotten; and, 2) once the State intervenes in an attempt to correct observable persistent injustices, the State presses on due to the reasonably-placed lack of trust that the balance of society will perform their roles as ordered by the Christian faith and taught by the Church. Business is viewed by the State as part of the problem; not as an essential part of the solution as the Church teaches (though, admittedly, this is not taught or shared well.) The setting aside of the ancient religion and the post-truth influence of the greater society and decreasing relevance of the Church are harbingers of the battle to which Christian business leaders, you and me, are called.

Social Justice vs. Socialism

The Church does not leave the answer to this predicament a mystery.

> The answer to this dilemma is the infusion of social justice and the sentiment of Christian love into the socio-economic order.[119] – Pope Pius XI

Although the Church has never proposed a definitive technical system, she has nevertheless clearly outlined the guiding principles which indicate the safe way of securing the happy progress of society.[120] The Church laments further. There are still too many people who are Catholic (Christian) in name only.[121] There is no manifestation of their faith and the tenets of the Gospel in their life outside of Mass or church service; much less at work. This absence of faith in the workplace contributes wholly to the exposure of man to the whims of business and ideologies contrary to human dignity and pursuit of the common good. Pope Pius XI stated it this way, "The Catholic who does not live really and sincerely according to the Faith he professes will not long be master of himself in these days when the winds of strife and persecution blow so fiercely, but will be swept away defenseless in this new deluge which threatens the world. And thus, while he is preparing his own ruin, he is exposing to ridicule the very name of Christian."[122] Absent a strong moral keel, the winds of the dominant culture prevail. The specter of socialism is arguably one giant step toward this new deluge and the ruin for which man is preparing. The ridicule of Christianity generated from the impact of the observable hypocrisy of many business leaders who profess the Christian faith yet do otherwise is worthy of more examination.

I trust any consideration you may have in favor of socialism is adequately addressed through the teachings of the Church. The Church leaves little room for anything other than rejection of the tenets thereof. But simultaneously, it demands the infusion of social justice and Christian love into the socio-economic order. Given the current inertia and force of the dominant ideology in business, many Christian business leaders have no idea where to begin. The parts of this book to follow will clarify what business in a well-functioning free market looks like and what business leaders can do in practice to bring to life a purpose of business that is higher still; transcendent, if you will; while building a more competitive and successful business enterprise measured using any traditional business metric of success you choose.

This book's section on Virtuosos provides some concrete examples of transcendent businesses and virtuous business leaders from whom you can learn and be inspired. And these are all remarkably successful and industry-leading businesses!

Chapter 3 Key Takeaways

1. In pursuit of the noble cause of social justice, people don't intend to give away their most basic freedoms. Yet those who see socialism as the answer for social justice do exactly that.

2. Ironically, the ultra-right-leaning conservatives' unforgiving grip on concepts like libertarianism and laissez-faire government, absent a fixed set of moral rules, has done more to stir the flames of socialism than other influences.

3. Debates around socialism are not about achieving the ends of social justice, but about the means used to achieve those ends.

4. Socialism is intrinsically wrong; incongruent with natural law; and, consequently, should be rejected as an answer to the question of social justice.

5. The State or government cannot lay claim to our own primary responsibility for protecting human rights and flourishing in the economic sector. That responsibility lies in the hands of the many who lead and groups who serve those working in business.

6. The Catholic Social Teaching concept of subsidiarity is best served when business leaders tend to their responsibility to protect human dignity and pursue the common good in and through business, leaving the government to do only what it can do and does well.

7. The Church suggests that the solution to social injustice in-lieu of socialism is to inject Christian love into the socio-economic sector (i.e., in business).

8. How do Christian love in business and the dominant ideology of the pursuit of maximizing profit coexist? Can they?

Chapter 3 Synopsis

While social justice is a worthy and noble cause, socialism is not the answer. Christian love in business is. This is what the Church teaches. Business leaders must tend to that primary role of protecting human dignity and the pursuit of the common good in and through business. Left to the government, the U.S. inches closer and closer to a devastating remodeling of government and society in the form of socialism.

CHAPTER 4

Free Markets and Truth

❧❧❧

IT IS HARD TO deny the Church's adamant stance against socialism even in the face of mounting dismissal of the Church as irrelevant by the greater culture. History's record of the moral consequences of socialism provide corroborating evidence of its inherent flaws that are wholly inconsistent with natural law and the morality of man. Marxism criticized capitalist bourgeois societies, blaming them for the commercialization and alienation of human existence. This rebuke is of course based on a mistaken and inadequate idea of alienation, derived solely from the sphere of relationships of production and ownership, that is, giving them a materialistic foundation and moreover denying the legitimacy and positive value of market relationships even in their own sphere. Marxism thus ends up by affirming that only in a collective society can alienation be eliminated. However, the historical experience of socialist countries has sadly demonstrated that collectivism does not do away with alienation but rather increases it, adding to it a lack of basic necessities and economic inefficiency.[123] One need only listen to or watch the news of human rights violations and the significant protests underway in China and Venezuela to know of the Marxist failure. If the people of North Korea were not so oppressed and their voices suppressed, we'd hear even more of the human tragedy born of a socialist state.

It is equally hard to deny, though, the Church's insistence on bringing Christian love and the infusion of social justice into the economic sector. History, too, is being written about the American Experiment with a Democratic government in which freedom and liberty are held in high regard, leveraging a free market economy where rule of law and the right to private property are sacrosanct, yet where morality is shifting and twisting, leaving the moral consequences of business still in question.

> **Christian business leaders will write the end of this story.**

So, where do we start? Michael Novak, in his book *Business as a Calling* writes:

> "In the project of self-government, business is without doubt the single largest institution of civil society. The moral health of society, therefore, depends to a great extent on the moral character of business leaders."[124]

I suggest that reconciling the tenets of a free market economy with the objective truth we know as Christians is an essential foundation on which to build our business practices, and more importantly, on which to define a purpose of business that is more accurate than that defined narrowly and simplistically by the current dominant ideology.

Is Capitalism the Answer?

Saint John Paul II pondered this question in his Encyclical Letter, *Centesimus Annus*, 42:

"Returning now to the initial question: can it perhaps be said that, after the failure of Communism, Capitalism is the victorious social system, and that Capitalism should be the goal of the countries now making efforts to rebuild their economy and society? Is this the model which ought to be proposed to the countries of the Third World which are searching for the path to true economic and civil progress?

The answer is obviously complex. If by "Capitalism" is meant an economic system which recognizes the fundamental and positive role of business, the market, private property and the resulting responsibility for the means of production, as well as free human creativity in the economic sector, then the answer is certainly in the affirmative, even though it would perhaps be more appropriate to speak of a "business economy", "market economy" or simply "free economy." But if by "Capitalism" is meant a system in which freedom in the economic sector is not circumscribed within a strong juridical framework which places it at the service of human freedom in its totality, and which sees it as a particular aspect of that freedom, the core of which is ethical and religious, then the reply is certainly negative."

A truly competitive market is an effective instrument for attaining important objectives of justice: moderating the excessive profits of individual businesses, responding to consumers' demands, bringing about a more efficient use and conservation of resources, rewarding entrepreneurship and innovation, making information available so that it is really possible to compare and purchase products in an atmosphere of healthy competition.[125] The Church's social doctrine, while recognizing the market as an irreplaceable instrument for regulating the inner workings of the economic system, points out the need for it to be firmly rooted in its ethical objectives, which ensure and at the same time suitably circumscribe the space within which it can operate autonomously.[126] So what are these ethical objectives of which the Church speaks in which the market is to be firmly rooted? Let's, again, seek truth for the answer.

Justice in a Free Market

Justice is one of four cardinal virtues from which all other virtues emanate. Justice is the moral virtue that consists in the constant and firm will to give their due to God and neighbor. Justice toward God is called the "virtue of religion." Justice toward men disposes one to respect the rights of each and to establish in human relationships the harmony that promotes equity with regard to persons and to the common good. The just man, often mentioned in the Sacred Scriptures, is distinguished by habitual right thinking and the uprightness of his conduct toward his neighbor.[127]

> More simply stated, justice consists in the firm and constant will to give God and neighbor their due.[128] – Catechism of the Catholic Church

The concept of justice harkens back to the answer recorded in *The Holy Bible* (NIV) when Jesus was asked, "Teacher, which is the greatest commandment in the Law?" Jesus replied, "Love the Lord your God with all your heart and with all your soul and with all your mind. This is the first and greatest commandment. And the second is like it: Love your neighbor as yourself. All the Law and the Prophets hang on these two commandments."[129] For the purpose of this writing, I'll leave the discussion of giving God justice or His due to the theologians, except to acknowledge its necessity in the overall formula for societal progress, success in business, and the Christ-centered life.

The ultimate question is this, "Can true justice be achieved in a free market economy, and if so, how?" There exist a few truths that are found in nature, and consequently, are common to anything that purports to be consistent with natural law. One of those truths relates to inequality. Not everything is equal in nature, and not everything is equal in a free market economy. Is it equality we are after or is it equity? Equality is self-explanatory, but equity is less so. Does equity fairly represent what is due our neighbor? For the purposes of this argument, I suggest that it does.

David Hume, a friend and colleague of Adam Smith, went so far as to correlate the virtue of justice (contrived by man) with the necessary pre-requisite of inequality. He argued that absent inequality, justice would not be necessary. While his arguments for justice are purely utilitarian and centered on honoring one's right to earn and hold private property, his understanding of inequality as a precursor to justice is accurate. We as Christians, though, have a more profound duty and motivation to give our neighbor his or her due.

> **Justice for Christians is animated by the belief that our neighbors, both friend and foe, are created in the image of God, and therefore, are worthy of what is due them; even given the inequality of skills, talents, gifts, and learned competencies born into and developed in each person.**

The free market cannot be judged apart from the ends that it seeks to accomplish and from the values that it transmits on a societal level. Indeed, the market cannot find in itself the principles for its legitimization; it belongs to the consciences of individuals and to public responsibility to establish a just relationship between means and ends.[130] The free market's legitimization will ultimately be determined by business leaders' identification of the ends and means to be used to achieve those ends. The inversion of the relationship between means and ends, however, can make it (the free market) degenerate into an inhuman and alienating institution, with uncontrollable repercussions.

> "The individual profit of an economic enterprise, although legitimate, must never become the sole objective."[131] – Pontifical Council for Justice and Peace

How is a business leader to reconcile this admonition with the current purpose-of-business dominant ideology categorically penned in a 1970 article by Milton Friedman for The New York Times Magazine entitled, *The Social Responsibility of Business is to Increase its Profits*? Have not the means and ends of a business enterprise in a free market gotten inverted here? Has not the legitimate profit from an economic enterprise become arguably the sole objective in business today? Would the audience of business on-lookers, arguably all the stakeholders of a business, discern the answer differently from the shareholders of a business today? Would this same audience judge the behavior of business leaders, and consequently the enterprise they lead, "just" in its attribution of business success and related wealth to all stakeholders in such a way to give each his or her due with equity in mind, not equality? I think not. The injustice that gives rise to the real specter of socialism today, a lagging indicator of injustice, is evidence enough of this judgment.

This existential paradox for business and business leaders demands more clarity and understanding, as if a bright light were to shine upon it. Truth has shown itself, if only it were not clouded by the institution of business whose end is profit, not purpose. Ignorant of Adam Smith's cautions or extravagant passions; the vices of greed, ambition, and vanity illuminated in his book *The Theory of Moral Sentiments*; business leaders face this conundrum with dread and uncertainty. Dread speaks to the anticipated pain and sacrifice revealed as the light of truth illuminates the true purpose of business, and uncertainty peeks out from its perch because many know not how to apply truth in the context of business. This ambiguity is truly a tyrant, with business leaders its unsuspecting object; maintaining the business status quo for fear of what is yet unknown while missing the unforeseen blessings that await. As toward any tyrant, we wait, we stall, we freeze; waiting for some indication that we are safe to move.

Adam Smith's Clarity on Mutually Beneficial Exchanges

Could it be that the same dance of sentiments that framed Adam Smith's perspective of virtue and morality also frames his perspective on commercial exchanges? If so, this is a key bridge from Smith's *Theory of Moral Sentiments* and more famous book and tenets that foretell why some nations are wealthier than others; *The Wealth of Nations*. Let's take look at commercial exchanges with the full backdrop of Smith's wisdom and insights on moral sentiments and the mutual desire for sympathy thereof.

> "At its essence, business is inherently others-centered."[132] – Pontifical Council for Justice and Peace

Business at its core must concern itself with unmet needs of society and, ultimately, with the needs of and means available to each individual consumer. As such, Smith might argue that a good business when left alone (like in a free market), without intervention (as in a laissez-faire or limited government) or incentive beyond our own self-interest, man will seek mutually beneficial exchanges; one where the product or service offered is valued and paid for at an equivalent price.

> **Much like the dance of sentiments, the give-and-take of a commercial transaction pushes and pulls until mutual benefit is reached.**

Contrarily, if an exchange is not considered mutually beneficial, and if the exchange is not forced, one will not execute the exchange until he or she believes they will recognize the anticipated equivalent benefit.

We can attest to the validity and reason of this framework simply by reflecting on our personal experience as buyers and sellers. Regularly, we exchange our hard-earned wages for goods and services. We do so willingly and often joyfully, anticipating the value we will receive from what we buy. The seller benefits from selling something we want, receiving the benefit of cash conversion and profit with which to care for his/her family, pay those he or she employs, invest in the community, or reinvest in more items to sell while we enjoy the value of the product or service purchased.

We also have the experience of seeing items where the price is too high to justify the purchase or the perceived quality of a product or service does not outweigh the money that would have to be exchanged. A business exchange is not consummated in these instances. The seller is free to sell his or her wares to the next buyer or adjust terms to try to sell their wares to me again; haggle, if you will. Likewise, the buyer is free to exchange his or her assets or cash with someone for something that is more valuable to him or her. In each circumstance, mutual benefit is a prerequisite.

> **What is equally, if not more informative are Smith's cautions of things that can pollute an environment designed for mutually beneficial exchanges, namely greed, ambition, and vanity.**

It is not hard to see economic transactions as mutually beneficial in this light. Nor is it hard to accept Adam Smith's notion of a free market and unencumbered economy with this insight. Had you not known more about Adam Smith's theory of moral sentiments, the role sympathies play and the dance thereof, it would be easy to conclude a more dubious defense of free markets, as many do.

Smith predictably fell short of prescribing an antidote with his ever-floating, others-influenced basis for morality. We will not make that same mistake for commercial exchanges. A nation that builds its economic system on private property rights and the rule of law without regard to a fixed set of moral laws or truth practiced by business leaders is doomed to an abusive, self-serving, common-good-diluted institution where injustice finds life and pride, greed, and envy; three of the seven deadly sins flourish.

Six Practical Principles for Business

With a secular perspective on mutually beneficial exchanges and a leaning toward a fixed set of moral laws, yet acknowledging our dread and uncertainty, let's look deeper into six practical principles for business that are endorsed by the Church. These principles, while practical, will at some point appear to **thrash** with the current dominant ideology and purpose of business to maximize shareholder wealth. What is meant by the term "thrash?" When clear but conflicting objectives exist, the objectives will cause friction and tension as they battle for attention and resources. We will refer to this tension and friction as "thrash."

As a business leader, for now, it is best to learn to live within this tension; between profit-generation and real purpose. As additional dots get connected in this book, we will see how real purpose and profit-generation co-exist and relate. For Christian business leaders, I often refer to this friction as the tension between piety and perversion. Knowing that this tight rope can be walked through my own experience, it does those of us believing in a fixed set of moral laws no good if we succumb to the temptation or 'perversion' of profit-generation as the ultimate end of a business, or if in our zealousness for our faith toward the real purpose of business, our 'piety' is so blinding that we are expelled from the marketplace for lack of demonstrable results.

> **We must walk within "what is" in order to bring about the transcendence that is "to be."**

A Christian business leader must first be governed by two preeminent and foundational principles of Catholic Social Teaching. These are respect for human dignity and pursuit of the common good. Absent these principles, it will be nearly impossible to climb out from the business rut we too often mistake for the horizon.

Practical Business Principle #1:
Deliver Good Products and Good Services

There is not a business in the world that is sustainable that does not meet a relevant need or want of another human being. Absent a relevant need or want, no business can survive. Yes, some of these desires can be misguided and even evil, but not withstanding this proper boundary, businesses naturally seek that which address these needs and does so in ever-creative and innovative ways, improving the value proposition to the market and the quality of life of individual customers and clients. This is the first and most fundamental practical principle: **Business must contribute to the common good by producing goods that are truly good and services that truly serve.**[133] Not much of a challenge here to Christian business leaders other than to ensure our products and services do not tempt or lead others into sin.

Practical Business Principle #2:
Serve the Poor and People in Need

This next practical principle is significantly more challenging. **Businesses must maintain solidarity with the poor by being alert for opportunities to serve deprived and underserved populations and people in need.**[134] In business, we tend to give significant attention to our paying customers and to our employees. This is where our proverbial bread is buttered, and these make logical and practical sense especially when we are trying to win in a competitive marketplace. These natural business priorities usually manifest in person-centric customer support, hiring the best candidate available within the appropriate range of compensation, and paying wages and benefits intended to recruit and retain those candidates as long-term employees. No challenge for existing businesses and Christian business leaders here either.

But what is a business to do if we must be on-point for opportunities to serve the poor? Might these be customers who cannot afford our product or service? What can we do for them without enabling or inviting an unhealthy dependency or creating a discount entitlement that even our paying customers would seek? What if this means not always hiring the best candidates, but the one or ones deserving of an opportunity to learn a skill and provide for their own families? Won't these things hurt our business? Do you feel the "thrash" or push against the dominant ideology here? This is where business leaders must climb out of the deep rut of the dominant purpose-of-business ideology to a purpose that is higher still.

Let's walk these ideas through some logical paths. First, who says we as Christian business leaders must concern ourselves with opportunities to serve the deprived, underserved, and marginalized people in need? This question is not unlike the question asked by the goats in Matthew 25, verse 44 (NIV): "Lord, when did we see you hungry or thirsty or a stranger or needing clothes or sick or in prison, and did not help you?" The reply comes immediately thereafter: "I tell you the truth, whatever you did not do for one of the least of these, you did not do for me." This scripture calls us to serve the least of these brothers because Christ is in them. You may say that I do these things with my wealth or earnings generated from the business. What is to be gained by my business concerning itself with these things if I already do it as an individual? This is a good question that warrants significantly more exploration.

> **I suggest to you that what is lost by your business by not doing these things is more important than what is to be gained.**

Perhaps an equally good question is if we don't do this as Christian business leaders, then who will? Think about the options. If we remain in the rut doing as we have always done; serving customers, hiring the best, and paying well for recruiting and retention purposes; those marginalized who can't afford, won't be hired, and won't be paid well enough to recruit or retain are left to fend for themselves or survive off the generosity of others. Well-to-do people will give generously to their chosen philanthropies or churches in hopes that their altruism will help cure the ills of those marginalized. The social distance between the deprived and the blessed remains vast and what should be a relationship of respect and humanity is simply transactional in nature; rendering some good; but falling well short of the love and charity expected of Christians of all traditions. As previously mentioned, this short-sighted charity of today is coined "secular humanitarianism." We give generously, yes, but too often keep our distance; lest we be seen as "unclean."

Another option is this. With the profits we reap from our competitive businesses, we'll pay taxes (though some will avoid this) and the State, exercising their necessary role as insurer and defender of human dignity and the pursuit of the common good, will intervene and establish a taxpayer funded program that likely creates, at best, an unhealthy dependency, and at worst, a long-lived entitlement mentality that perpetuates taxation of profitable companies and well-to-do individuals. This is logically what happens when we do not concern ourselves with the deprived, underserved, and marginalized people in society. The Catholic Social Teaching principle of subsidiarity is violated here. Look at government programs today for substantial evidence of this. **This is not what the Church supports.**

These opportunities to serve the poor, the deprived, or the marginalized can manifest through business-funded skills training programs to move those whose environments or lack of educational resources in formative years did not produce necessary skill sets required for gainful employment. They can manifest in intentional apprenticeships for trained craftsmen and women. They can manifest in employing the hard-to-hire or ex-offenders who need a chance to earn and restore their lives and families. They can manifest is manufacturing facilities in destitute areas that create employment and help spin-up economic development that has waned. They can manifest in bartering programs that allow those who can't afford a product or service to exchange their time and talent for the service to protect their dignity. They can manifest in "bottom of the pyramid" products and services such as microenterprises, microcredit, and impact investment funds.[135]

> **As Christian business leaders, we are limited only by our lack of imagination and by what we believe is the purpose of our business.**

Practical Business Principle #3:
Foster and Offer the Dignity of Human Work

Work is intended for the person and not the other way around.[136] Employees are not mere "human resources" or "human capital." Consequently, work must be designed for the capacities and qualities of human beings.[137] The way human work is designed and managed has a significant impact on whether an organization can compete in the marketplace and whether people will flourish through their work.[138] **Business makes a contribution to the community by fostering the special dignity of human work.**[139] This can be seen vividly today in businesses and through business leaders who are progressive in their management and leadership practices. These forerunners know that their employees make the difference between success and failure and they invest heavily in their competence to breed confidence; allowing them to flourish and grow while at work.

Unfortunately, there exist a number of business managers and leaders who don't trust others and significantly limit employees' potential with arbitrary rules and approvals and ambiguous expectations that relegate workers to mindless automatons pandering to every momentary pang of their leaders. The indignity suffered by these workers is not the vision foreseen and expected by the Church. Because work changes the person, it can enhance or suppress that person's dignity; it can allow a person to develop or be damaged.

Good work gives scope for the intelligence and freedom of workers; it promotes social relationships and real collaboration; and it does not damage the health and physical well-being of the worker, let alone spiritual well-being and religious freedom. Moreover, reward structures should make sure that those workers who do engage their labor in a sincere way also receive the necessary esteem and compensation from their companies.[140] These elements are common in business leaders who are more progressive in their management and leadership practices, absent perhaps the lesser-observed scope of spiritual well-being and religious freedom.

Practical Business Principle #4:
Offer Employees Greater Opportunities for Contributions

This principle is closely related to the previously mentioned practical business principle; foster the special dignity of human work but is more instructional in its expectation. The Catholic Social Teaching principle of subsidiarity is honored through this expectation. Subsidiarity is rooted in the conviction that, as images of God, the flourishing of human beings entails the best use of employees' gifts and freedom. Human dignity is never respected by unnecessarily constraining or suppressing gifts or freedom. Subsidiarity insists that the gifts and freedom of those closest to the effects to be felt should not be arbitrarily disregarded.[141] Employees should have a voice in their work, especially in the day-to-day work. This fosters initiative, innovation, creativity and a sense of shared responsibility.[142] Does this not sound like the progressive practice of empowering employees and creating progressive work environments where employees can be self-directed?!

> "Business should embrace subsidiarity providing opportunities for employees to exercise their gifts as they contribute to the mission of the organization."[143] – Pontifical Council for Justice and Peace

The principle of subsidiarity also encourages business leaders to use their power at the service of everyone in their organization and prompts them to question whether their authority serves the development of all their employees. The progressive management and intrinsic motivation elements of autonomy and self-mastery are served well through the principle of subsidiarity.

> At the end of the day, people are not means to be used to achieve the ends of profit in business. The people in business are ends in-and-of themselves.

Practical Business Principle #5:
Be Good Stewards of all Resources

Good stewards are not just takers and consumers of resources; be those capital, human, or environmental resources. Good stewards create and devise ways to replace, if not grow what has been given to them. **Business should model stewardship of all resources – whether capital, human, or environmental – under their control.**[144] Financial profit is one measure of multiplying capital resources. The Church acknowledges the legitimate role of profit as an indicator that a business is functioning well. When a firm makes a profit, it generally means that the factors of production have been properly employed and corresponding human needs have been duly satisfied.[145] There is little debate that profit obtained legally, through real value provided, bought and sold through proper channels, made and sold ethically, and earned through mutually beneficial exchanges serves to improve the well-being of those in the business, arguably at differing levels, and serves to improve the well-being of those in the communities in which a business employs people and in which it sells its wares.

"A profitable business, by creating wealth and promoting prosperity, helps individuals excel and realize the common good of society."[146] – Pontifical Council for Justice and Peace

The economic value of profit or wealth is inextricably linked, though, to a wider notion of well-being.[147] This wider notion of well-being includes the physical, mental, psychological, moral and spiritual well-being of others.[148] Thrash. As ends in-and-of themselves, the people entrusted to our care and development as business leaders deserve our best effort and investment, not just in utilitarian business and economic terms because caring for people is "good business," but because work was created for man; not vice versa. With this focus on people as ends, business is expected to foster the special dignity of human work and the related shepherding of the human beings participating therein.

Practical Business Principle #6:
Justly Distribute Rewards to all Stakeholders

Thrash. While serving the poor and deprived in-and-through business challenges many of our thoughts about business and its ultimate purpose, there is nothing quite so explicitly counter-cultural as the idea that the rewards of the business should be distributed justly. **Business should be just in its allocation of benefits to all stakeholders: employees, customers, investors, suppliers, and the community.**[149] The dominant ideology coupled with the primacy of shareholders today would indicate that benefits, chief among them being profit, should be the propriety of shareholders alone. This has become such an enduring norm that stock ownership in the form of options – a long-standing privilege of investors – are now the incentive of choice for executives and middle-managers of many business firms to allow them to participate in the benefits or profit of the business. This norm has had serious unintended consequences. Coupled with the financialization of the economy centered on profit and return on capital invested, this norm has created the breeding ground for immense moral dilemmas in business.

> **The primacy of shareholders combined with the purpose of business to maximize shareholder wealth has created a toxic cocktail that has been the demise of many prevailing businesses and talented business leaders while tainting the pool of business for those of us who remain.**

Enron and its stakeholders fell victim to it. WorldCom and Health South, among many others, likewise fell.

If one accepts that God's creation is intended for everyone – rich and poor, powerful and weak, now and in the future (mirroring the Catholic Social Teaching principle of universal destination of goods, to which the right to private ownership of property is subordinated), then it follows business decisions should aim not at an equal, but a just distribution of wealth that meets people's needs, rewards their contributions and risks, and preserves and promotes the organization's financial health.[150] Herein lies the argument for a livable wage, shared ownership, and other progressive pressures in the modern day workplace. The Church is not blind to the reality that a business is limited in its just distribution to that which would put the enterprise at risk of survival.[151]

This boundary is an invitation for business leaders to consider where in the range of distribution (from survival-only on one extreme and shareholder-only on the other) are rewards and benefits distributed justly. Again, there is plenty of room for creativity and innovation by business leaders to determine where and how to best accomplish this. You will find examples of how some companies and business leaders have done this in the section of this book entitled Virtuosos.

Now educated with the truth as the Church would define it for business, we can no longer plead ignorance. This may feel heavy to you, though, for some of you this may feel light – just as Jesus shared in Matthew 11:30 (NIV), "For my yoke is easy and my burden is light." Perhaps you now have some insight into what business should be that remedies your struggle to reconcile your faith and truth with what-is in business.

> **Free markets and truth go together, as do faith and reason.**

We can either take up our cross in business and practice these truths, or we can succumb to the inertia of business as it is today; leaving social justice in the hands of the State, supported by growing numbers of those who observe no better option and who push for an entire reshaping of government and society. By taking up our cross in business, business becomes transcendent. Thrash. What will you do with this truth? Too often, we as Christians are educated way beyond our obedience, and much is at stake.

Chapter 4 Key Takeaways

1. The moral health of society depends significantly on the moral health of business and its leaders. I'm fond of saying in leadership circles that there is no such thing as unhealthy organizations, only unhealthy people. Organizations don't behave. People do.

2. Capitalism or a free economy is preferred, if it is subordinated to the pursuit of human freedom in its entirety; the core of which is ethical and religious.

3. The cardinal virtue of justice is demanded in free markets warranting that each person is due what is his or hers based simply on being created in the image of God. This is much more substantial than Hume's secular perspective on justice.

4. Business is inherently others-centered. The application of Smith's desire for mutual sympathy in sentiments and

mutually beneficial exchanges can be applied to employer and employee relationships.

5. People are ends in-and-of themselves, not merely means to be used in pursuit of profit.

6. The Church offers six practical principles of business:
    a. Produce goods and good services.
    b. Serve the poor and people in need through business.
    c. Foster and offer the dignity of human work.
    d. Offer employees greater opportunities to contribute.
    e. Steward resources well.
    f. Distribute rewards justly.

7. Shareholder primacy can no longer be the norm, though they deserve consideration as a key stakeholder, as do employees, vendors, and our communities.

8. Businesses should practice justice up-and-to the point of putting the enterprise itself at risk. There likely exists plenty of margin between what is practiced today benefiting a few and what could be benefiting many without putting a business at risk.

Chapter 4 Synopsis

The truth and teaching of the Church are aligned with well-functioning free markets, but the purpose of business must change to that which focuses on people as ends in-and-of themselves. Giving each person in business his or her due manifests the virtue of justice in the marketplace. The practice of justice is bound to that which does not put the business itself at risk.

CHAPTER 5

Virtue in the Marketplace

❦

"Those who rule the commonwealths should avail themselves of the laws and institutions of the country; masters and wealthy owners must be mindful of their duty; the working class, whose interests are at stake, should make every lawful and proper effort; and since religion alone, as we said at the beginning, can avail to destroy the evil at its root, all men should rest persuaded that that main thing needful is to re-establish Christian morals, apart from which all the plans and devices of the wisest will prove of little avail." - Pope Leo XIII in his Encyclical Letter *Rerum Novarum*, 62.

IT IS LIKELY THAT your dread and uncertainty may have peaked, perhaps in contrast to the excitement of what could-be in business when the reason of a free market meets truth in the form of our Christian faith. This insight and excitement are a powerful force in the hands and hearts of Christian business leaders. We as business leaders are not immune from the human tendency to choose pain avoidance over the most gain, though. The obstacles and inertia against this movement are substantial, and not all these forces are of this earth or physical obstacles. (For our struggle is not against flesh and blood, but against the rulers, against the authorities, against the powers of this dark world and against the spiritual forces of evil in the heavenly realms. *Ephesians 6:12* NIV) On what, then, can we lean and from what can we learn to help fuel our drive toward that purpose in business that is higher still?

Christian virtues are our lever and our light. Everyone who claims Christianity as his or her faith is called to live a virtuous life. *The Holy Bible* (RSV) book of Wisdom 8:7 records, "And if anyone loves righteousness, her labors are virtues; for she teaches self-control and prudence, justice and courage; nothing in life is more profitable for men than these."[152]

> "A virtue is a habitual and firm disposition to do the good. It allows the person not only to perform good acts, but to give the best of himself. The virtuous person tends toward the good with all his sensory and spiritual powers; he pursues the good and chooses it in concrete actions."[153] – Catechism of the Catholic Church

Furthermore, human virtues are firm attitudes, stable dispositions, habitual perfections of intellect and will that govern our actions, order our passions, and guide our conduct according to reason and faith. They make possible ease, self-mastery, and joy in leading a morally good life. The virtuous man is he who freely practices the good.[154] Herein lies the keel that allows us Christian business leaders to turn our business ship safely toward transcendence and keep it on course against the winds, waves, and currents that beg otherwise. Christian virtues are a critical manifestation of fixed moral laws; the third leg of the well-functioning free market stool.

But living virtuously is not easy. I repeat a question that Robert Heilbroner, an author and student of Adam Smith posited, "How can human beings, who are presumably captives to their own self-interest, suspend selfish considerations to form disinterested 'moral' judgments?[155] It is not easy for man, wounded by sin, to maintain moral balance. Christ's gift of salvation offers us the grace necessary to persevere in the pursuit of the virtues.[156] Absent the ancient religion set aside by public institutions and the law and too often invisible in business today, other efforts will prove of little-to-no avail, as quoted at the opening of this chapter. I choose the aforementioned words carefully. The term "set aside" was the term chosen by Pope Leo XIII in his foundational Encyclical Letter, *Rerum Novarum*, in paragraph 3, where I suggest he defined the core problem facing business in the laissez-faire government days of the European Industrial Revlution:

> "Public institutions and the laws set aside the ancient religion. Hence, by degrees it has come to pass that working men have been surrendered, isolated and helpless, to the hardheartedness of employers and the greed of unchecked competition."[157]

> **If business is to become transcendent, then we can no longer ignore and set aside that which propels us toward the good and toward God; a life of virtue at work.**

If living a life of virtue is the critical manifestation of a fixed set of moral rules in a well-functioning free market, then it would do us well to know of, learn about, and practice the virtues of which we speak. The Church has identified two formal categories of virtues: cardinal virtues and theological virtues. Cardinal virtues are so named as they are the four virtues from which all others emanate.

> **The cardinal virtues are prudence or wisdom, temperance, justice, and fortitude or courage.**

The three theological virtues help Christ-followers to perfect other virtues. They are the foundation of Christian moral activity;

they animate it and give it its special character. They inform and give life to all the moral virtues. They are infused by God into the souls of the faithful . . . They are the pledge of the presence and action of the Holy Spirit in the faculties of the human being. The theological virtues are faith, hope, and charity or love.[158]

Virtue is not the trailhead of Christians alone. All people can choose to practice prudence, justice, temperance, and courage and some who are not Christian do. You can see it in their generosity, humility, passion, and character. So why can't I as a business leader just practice these virtues outside of the Christian faith? You can, but what truly animates and gives power to Christians choosing to practice virtue are the perfecting theological virtues of faith, hope, and love. Living our faith, knowing and abiding in scripture, asking for and receiving ancient wisdom, and believing that eternity is our destination; not this life; give the Christian business leader the deep roots and courage to withstand the battering from the greater culture and the fight and stamina to win the race. Nothing is stronger in the face of evil or animus than a virtuous Christian who knows of and seeks their eternal destination. Keep the energizing and animating theological virtues of faith, hope, and love in mind as you learn more about the cardinal virtues.

The Cardinal Virtues Applied to Business

Prudence

Prudence or wisdom is the virtue that disposes practical reason to discern our true good in every circumstance and to choose the right means of achieving it. It is prudence that immediately guides the judgment of conscience. With the help of prudence, we apply moral principles to particular cases without error and overcome doubts about the good to achieve and the evil to avoid.[159] By design and definition, the consequence of prudence is more than knowing what is right. It's a choice to do the right thing. As such, prudence guides the other virtues by setting rule and measure.[160]

> **Without prudence, as already set forth in this book, we are left with an amorphous morality from which to draw choices and actions of right and wrong.**

Business creates a unique set of "particular cases" to which prudence or wisdom applies. In a world where moral relativism lives and good and evil are individual filters, this virtue is critically important and provides the foundation on which the fixed set of moral laws rests. Otherwise, what would be wisdom is simply that to which society would agree is tolerable, leaving truth wanting and free markets in danger. A floating and amorphous morality makes the dominant ideology in business an acceptable alternative to what should be in business. Prudence would cause one to question that narrow field of vision and cause one to make business decisions appropriate to and aligned with the different, if not the divine end of business; that of transcendence.

Here are a few insights forwarded from the Virtuosos chapter of this book, in which we share industry-leading company stories, their values, and their business practices that evidence these virtues. You'll notice that, though we are starting with the virtue of prudence, many actions as a consequence of prudence overlap with the other virtues. While we talk about each virtue separately, the individual virtues are less silos than interdependent forces that move us toward holiness. Here are some examples of the virtue of prudence in business application:

Onyx Collection – Leaders here do not seek exclusivity, intellectual property protections, or market dominance aspirations common to most businesses. Prudence tells them that exclusivity and monopolistic-type behaviors trigger competitive animus and put true competition at risk (through unnatural and administrative veils). They believe letting the best company win, absent common protections, is the best way for both the business and employees to flourish.

Tim Haahs – Core values here demand that all incoming calls be returned the same day and that all stakeholders are informed of their entire project – good or bad. In professional service firms like engineering and architecture, communication is not the strong suit of professionals doing the work, yet prudence dictates this to be right, appropriate, and a competitive advantage that raises the performance bar for employees and enhances service to their customers.

Temperance

Temperance is the moral virtue that moderates the attraction of pleasures and provides balance in the use of created goods. It ensures the will's mastery over instincts and keeps desires within the limits of what is honorable.[161] Everything in moderation is a very practical application of this virtue. Temperance helps us reduce reliance on the world's goods. This virtue is especially profound to those in and leading business as the rewards thereof can be substantial. These rewards that many others cannot afford make pleasures and goods tempting to business leaders.

> **Our ignorance of temperance results in consumerism and excess wealth being used for frivolous purposes, not for investment in people and not toward pursuit of the common good.**

Here are a few insights forwarded from the Virtuosos chapter revealing the virtue of temperance. Keep in mind the interdependent forces previously mentioned:

Compass Financial Resources – Leaders here built enough trust among producers for them to give up their individual commission checks (a compensation norm in the financial advising industry that is not aligned with any form of teamwork and often misaligned with client best interests), risking earning less to produce a better and more comprehensive result for customers. This risk paid off and producers now earn 4-5x what they earned individually. Lack of concern for self and setting aside personal ambitions and wealth that could be used for personal gain yielded bigger gains for all.

Tim Haahs – Prior to the sub-prime mortgage crash, the firm set aside cash reserves (millions of dollars) over several years with an anticipation to preserve employment of professionals in case of a market disruption. This move, sacrificing current disposable income and personal wealth-building in the present, allowed the firm to sustain, survive, and then grow on the heels of the 2008 recession. When other businesses disappeared on the heels of the recession, Tim Haahs prevailed and grew thereafter.

Justice

Following prudence and temperance in this order for logic purposes only, justice as already addressed herein, concerns itself with the human dignity of each person and the due each person deserves as one created in the image of God. Justice is the moral virtue that consists in the constant and firm will to give due to God and to neighbor. Justice towards men disposes one to respect the rights of each and to establish in human relationships the harmony that promotes equity with regard to persons and to the common good.[162]

In business, justice demands that business leaders concern themselves with the lives of those with whom they have been entrusted, namely their employees. This concern is not uncommon in any business, but the motive may be substantially different. Caring for employees is good business! It makes sense regardless of why you do it.

> Yet, when justice is animated by the moral obligation Christian business leaders have, justice is never left wanting and comes in many creative and meaningful ways; not the least of these are often shared ownership, profit-sharing, gain-sharing, and generous spontaneous rewards made available through value creation and the resulting wealth generation.

Here are a few insights forwarded from the Virtuosos chapter evidencing the virtue of justice, among others:

Onyx Collection – 100% of health insurance premiums for all employees and family members are paid by the company. No employees share in these costs and there is no differentiation in participation between management and employees. This acknowledges that each employee and their family is due this benefit without regard to position or status. They receive this benefit simply because they are employees.

Tim Haahs – The firm is hard to compete with in their area of specialty: designing, engineering, and constructing parking and mixed-use structures. They have some history of sharing awarded contracts with the competing firms who lost the contract to them for the purpose of helping competitors survive and retain their people.

Fortitude

Fortitude is the moral virtue that ensures firmness in difficulties and constancy in the pursuit of the good. It strengthens the resolve to resist temptations and to overcome obstacles in the moral life. The virtue of fortitude enables one to conquer fear and to face trials and persecutions.[163] And in business, swimming upstream against the dominant ideology, you are highly likely to face trials and obstacles. By the world's standards these are mild forms of persecution, yet persecution none-the-less.

> **There is little doubt that courage is required to allow you to persevere when you carry the flag of free markets with truth as its mast.**

Here are a few insights forwarded from the Virtuosos chapter evidencing the virtue of fortitude:

Tim Haahs – On a parking garage project, load-bearing columns were found to not be reinforced with steel as required by code.

Though the firm prepared the engineering plans properly, it was a mistake by the construction contractor. Without delay or concern for the money to be spent, the firm helped the client find a carbon-fiber wrap solution that saved the client project and the construction company their reputation and liability.

Onyx Collection – The company does not believe in marketing and commits itself to letting its performance and value proposition spread through word-of-mouth channels only.

Reclaiming truth in the marketplace where mutually beneficial exchanges come freely will require business leaders to practice these virtues. Do you see the creativity in the Virtuoso companies and the virtues shining through from the leaders therein? This can feel overwhelming and seem insurmountable, but recall the option if we continue down the path free markets and capitalism are on today, the intrusiveness of government, and the specter of socialism on the horizon. The relevant question, again, is what will we as Christian business leaders choose?

Wealth and the Critical Choice in Business

Our choice will write (and right) the end of this story. Here's how. In a free market economy, much like that existing in the U.S., people are significantly free to produce and deliver products or services within the constraints of the rule of law, in hopes of securing private property with which to care for themselves, their families, and their neighbors. This natural force of self-interest, not selfishness (self-interest born of bad intentions), catalyzes creativity and innovation for ever-improving products and services to be sold in the free market. Consequently, consumers benefit from improved value, and for that improved value, consumers gladly exchange their hard-earned wages or property for goods and service. [Hold a marker here for those whose earnings do not allow them to participate in these exchanges. These are the people pushed to and left at the margin of society.]

It follows that the business or that community of persons[164] who is most creative and innovative in their product and services or produces the most value, consequently, likely garners the most margin between what is sold and the expenses incurred to create and deliver their product or service. A broad indicator of this value is profit, and accumulated profit is wealth. The more value created; the more wealth generated in business.

> **Here originates what is arguably the Christian businessperson's most blinding and absorbing challenge: what to do with that wealth.**

If the businessperson keeps the wealth for him or herself, which is wholly consistent with the dominant ideology of business today and very tempting, these Bible verses speak to the consequences.

- ➤ Matthew 6:24 (NIV), "No one can serve two masters. Either he will hate the one and love the other, or he will be devoted to the one and despise the other. You cannot serve both God and Money."
- ➤ 1 Timothy 6:10 (RSV), "For the love of money is the root of all evils . . ."
- ➤ Mark 10:25 (NIV), "It is easier for a camel to go through the eye of a needle than for a rich man to enter the kingdom of God."
- ➤ James 1:10-11 (NIV), "But the one who is rich should take pride in his low position, because he will pass away like a wildflower. For the sun rises with scorching heat and withers the plant; its blossom falls and its beauty is destroyed. In the same way, the rich man will fade away even while he goes about his business."

Remember, the Church endorses the idea of profit as an indication that a business is providing value and using its resources effectively and efficiently. That is not the problem. It's what we choose to do with the accumulated wealth that is in question.

> **If we keep excess capital earned for our own benefit and leave to the State the role of ensuring the respect for the human dignity of those pushed to the margin of society and pursuit of the common good, we are inviting the tide of sentiment favoring socialism.**

Without another option, the State is seen as the Savior, and as presented in this book, socialism and its minions are antithetical to truth.

A well-functioning free market absent a fixed set of moral laws to inform the purpose of business or commerce, and the lack of virtue practiced by business leaders demanded within the Christian faith reveal a paradoxical governing dynamic to which businesses are subject. It starts with the business leader's choice of vice over virtue. If we business leaders are not prudent, just, temperate, and courageous with the accumulated wealth generated from our businesses, then government is forced to ensure the protection of human dignity and pursuit of the common good in the economic sector. Insuring is the State's role, but it is not on whom the primary responsibility rests. That responsibility rests with us.[165]

As an indirect employer, with no revenue other than that collected from taxing those who earn, the government, a higher-order entity, will build programs to supplement that which was intended to be accomplished by a lower-order entity; the organization or enterprise of business (think subsidiarity). These programs tend to create unhealthy dependencies that perpetuate their existence often well beyond their need, against the teaching of the Church or truth. The taxation of profits funding these programs results in reduced investment, reduced spending, mischievous activities to avoid taxes, and other non-value add activities that serve to reduce creativity, innovation, and value creation; reducing wealth generation that when subject to vice, demands more State intervention . . . and the cycle continues.

> ## The hoarding of capital logically follows and the economic and social distance of those who-have increases over those who have-not.

An economy spirals downward; all on the heels of business leaders choosing vice over virtue. This might be illustrated like this:

© 2015 Dave Geenens

You may argue that if this is so, then why is our economy so strong so often in the U.S.? There are certainly areas of the economy and people therein benefiting, but it's hard to ignore the tension building in the tectonic plates ungirding our economy in the U.S. and the discussion of socialist tendencies as a lagging indicator of injustice. Are we as business leaders to whitewash what we now know to be true about people being more than just means to an end with human flourishing an outcome of business? Are we going to continue to ignore Holy Scripture or are we going to lead a transcendent business that places capitalism or a free market within the framework of human freedom in its totality and animate the core of this freedom which is ethical or religious?

Before we explore what happens if business leaders choose the latter, let's wrap-up our discussion of what happens in a free market when business leaders choose vice or don't choose virtue. This choice unveils a governing dynamic to which businesses in a free market are subject:

> **The level of government intervention is inversely proportional to the level of virtue practiced in business.**

Choosing materialism and consumerism over temperance; choosing folly over wisdom; choosing inequity over justice; and choosing fear over courage brings with it State intervention, intrusion, and overreach. If you don't like this trend, then perhaps you need to examine the other path aligned with truth, choosing virtue over vice.

Chapter 5 Key Takeaways

1. Choose the most gain over reduced pain; a choice not often made. Virtue is both our lever and our light as Christians.
2. Just because the public institutions and greater culture have set aside the ancient religion does not mean we as Christian businessmen and women need to set aside our faith and our belief systems.
3. Contrarily, it is essential that we Christian business leaders take up our cross and pursue a life of virtue – consistently practicing the good in business, among other life contexts.
4. The virtues from which all others emanate or cardinal virtues are prudence or wisdom, justice, temperance, and fortitude or courage.

5. The virtues are made more perfect through the practice of the three theological virtues: faith, hope, and charity or love. These perfecting and animating virtues give the Christian business leaders their unique and God-sized power.

6. In business, wisdom or prudence allows us to know what is right or good and to act upon that good. Prudence is essential to the fixed set of moral laws incumbent to a well-functioning free market. Imagine how imperfect prudence is without faith, hope, and love, the three theological virtues.

7. Temperance in business helps us to reduce our reliance on the goods of this world manifested in less materialism and more storing up treasures in heaven where moth and rust don't destroy (Matthew 6:19 NIV).

8. Justice imposes upon the business practitioner that each man or woman working on, in, or for the business receive that which is his or her due, simply because they are created in the image of God.

9. Courage or fortitude is required to persevere through trials and tribulations when taking such bold steps to return to the true purpose of business which is about human flourishing.

10. Wealth is a consequence of value creation and value creation is a function of meeting an unmet need well. These are all made possible in a free market. The primary problem arises when a business leader is faced with what to do with this wealth.

11. Businesspeople can choose either vice or virtue. Choosing vice renders the State as insurer to protect human dignity and pursue the common good, yet it is not the State's primary responsibility. That responsibility lies with us.

12. The level of government intervention is inversely proportional to the level of virtue practiced in business. If you don't like intrusive and heavy-handed and inefficient government intervention, then practice virtue in business. The State acts when we don't.

Chapter 5 Synopsis

Practicing virtue is an essential part of transitioning a business and its intentions toward transcendence. The core problem rests in setting aside the ancient religion. To correct this mistake, we must take up our cross as business leaders and practice the cardinal virtues perfected by the theological virtues. When we do, we reduce the level of government intervention and allow our free market to function well for the benefit of everyone.

CHAPTER 6

Virtuous Leadership and Employment

ᖴᖱᖹ

"RIGHTING" THE END TO this story begins here. Now educated of the alignment of the truth of our faith with the reason of free markets, let's explore what happens when business leaders choose virtue over vice. Something amazing happens! But we need to understand more about leadership at its core to appreciate and embrace this phenomenon. Unfortunately, some that has been written about leadership in business, much of which is good and instructional, has served to dilute leadership to the idea that everyone is a leader. This simply is not true. Yes, anyone can lead, but make no mistake; leading is a conscious choice to lead and commitment to that which causes others to follow. Until you make this choice, you are not a leader. Patrick Lencioni, in his book *The Motive*, argues additionally that it is not simply the choice, but your motivation behind the choice to lead. Are you choosing leadership to reap the prestige, the status, and the rewards thereof? Or are you choosing leadership for the responsibility and, often, the sacrifice of self for the benefit of others? You are invited to examine your conscience around these questions.

One of the leadership diluting and damaging ideas is that of self-leadership. Proponents indicate that leadership begins with self-leadership. I understand their emphasis here, but I refer to this as self-discipline, not leadership.

> **Self-discipline is no doubt a pre-requisite for leadership, but it is not leadership.**

Just because you can do the work and model it, does not mean others will follow. Of course, if you are not willing to do the work, then you can bet no one will follow you except through coercive means, which is not leadership.

To get to leadership at its core, let's apply the Theory of Constraints celebrated in the books *The Goal* and *Velocity*; two books I highly recommend reading. The premise in the book *Velocity* is that optimizing everything does not mean everything is optimized. This is not just a play on words or paradox. The Theory of Constraints (ToC) holds that in any process and at any given time, there is only one constraint that limits the throughput of the process. Optimizing that one constraint is critical, while making other process areas equally productive is a waste of resources and effort.

This is true for individual work as a process, too. Try this exercise. Watch someone work alone and see if you can identify the obstacles to accomplishing the work he or she is doing. What is the limiting obstacle or constraint? Is it inertia requiring force to move his or her body, or physical force enough to move an object? Is it sensory in order to navigate a walking/working path without harm to oneself or others? The ToC would recommend that once the process constraint is identified, two things should happen to increase the throughput of the work or process: 1) optimize the constraint – meaning make sure the element, machine, workstation, or energy is continuously on or open, with no downtime, and 2) subordinate everything else: the other work, other machines, other processes, or other places energy is spent to the constraint. Don't worry about other elements, just focus on the constraint. Try this and observe several people working alone. What are the constraints you see?

Now, if you can, ask the one doing the work to do work that is impossible to accomplish independently or alone. For example, you might ask the person to lift and move a 500 lb. piece of equipment, or a complete skid of material without a hand truck. Like you did above, observe for obstacles. Watch them attempt to do the work by themselves for a moment. What's the limiting constraint now? Is it the equipment to be moved? The skid? They are too heavy. STOP.

You have just witnessed the truth, the core, the reason, and the rationale for leadership, yet you may not know it yet. The work you designed or asked to be accomplished could not be performed by one person. That person is likely frustrated and maybe even angry. If you recall, Hume referred to this state of the lone working man as "savage and solitary." Imagine if you were the person doing the work. Now the work requires more than just you. When this happens, the object of the work; the equipment or the skid; is no longer the constraint.

> **The constraint moved from the object of the work to your ability to get someone to help or cooperate with you in the work at hand.**

This constraint, when the work requires more than just you, is the moment leadership is required. Leadership is not required if the work requires just you. Recall our discussion of self-discipline as a pre-requisite to leadership, but not leadership.

This core, reason, and rationale for leadership also has its root in *The Holy Bible* in Ecclesiastes 4:9 (NIV), "Two are better than one, because they have a good return for their labor." The RSV Bible uses the terms "good reward for their toil" in the same chapter and verse. Faith meets reason here. If any two of us were to work together at a task, whatever it might be, it is likely the two of us would accomplish more than any single person if we work together and cooperate. This truth and reason changes everything for the business leader! As the

ToC suggests, once the limiting constraint is identified, optimize the constraint – in this case, optimize getting others to cooperate in the business, and subordinate everything else to it; let nothing hinder you or take precedence over this. This makes leadership absolutely essential to any business that requires more than one person.

> **At its essence, leadership is the art of optimizing cooperation.**

Being an effective business leader, expecting leadership of others, and holding yourself and others accountable for the practice thereof is your top priority in any business, because it is the ultimate limiting constraint regardless of the type of business you are in or the nature or object of the work. In this light, business leadership and virtue are now beautifully aligned! Would you be willing to follow and commit more fully and willingly to the work at hand if your leader were virtuous; where he or she chose wisdom over folly, moderation over materialism, justice over injustice, and courage over cowardice; all perfected by the virtues of faith, hope, and charity or love? I believe most would answer yes to this question.

> **And so it follows that a business leader who chooses virtue over vice creates an environment for employees, suppliers, and other stakeholders to commit more fully and willingly to what the business needs and the work.**

This is real competitive advantage! When people commit more fully and willingly to the work at hand, the cooperative constraint is overcome, the throughput of the business is optimized, and more value is created. When more value is created, more wealth is generated, and we end up at the same fork in the road; will we choose virtue or choose vice? Generally speaking, the more wealth generated, the more virtue is required to overcome the temptation of pleasures and goods. When business leaders make a choice for virtue over vice, their business and the entire economy spirals up, with reduced levels of government intervention because those on which the responsibility for respect for human dignity and the pursuit of the common good primarily rests are owning it. That's the business leader; you and me. This choice is illustrated below:

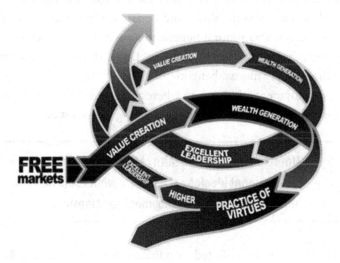

© 2015 DAVE GEENENS

Where is your dread and uncertainty now as it relates to the alignment of truth, virtue, and free markets? This will still demand courage, but the one life you've been given calls you to this; to build a competitive, growing and transcendent business that places people and their flourishing at the center of your effort; producing good goods and good services; providing good and productive work; and justly rewarding those who commit their limited time, talent, and learned capabilities to the effort at hand.

Mutual Benefit of Employment Relationships

With the confidence of truth and our faith now aligned with the reason of free markets, the practice of virtue essential to effective business leadership, and the centrality of employer/employee relationships to optimizing cooperation and competitive advantage, let's explore the mutual benefit of employment relationships. Are not employment relationships like mutually beneficial exchanges of products and services for value? We offer our muscle, our time, our skills, and our ability to learn, think, and obey for a wage. Our right to work is fulfilled and our time, skills, and obedience fulfill the needs of a business. Is not this mutual benefit the desired state of employer/employee relationships in a free market? Do truth and virtue demand more than simply mutual benefit?

In employment relationships where a free market for talent exists, let's assume mutual benefit is the underlying desired state.

> **Unfortunately, an unhealthy blind obedience to the dominant ideology can pollute what could be mutually beneficial employment relationships.**

At the core of polluted conditions for employer/employee exchanges is the abuse of and/or pursuit of power. Who holds the power in an employer/employee relationship? Power is slowly shifting, but in history employers or capitalists have wielded significant power over employees. This history reveals that employees often opted for dangerous low-paying jobs offered by employers to mitigate subsistence existence. Today, this might look like underemployment or gig-economy employment where with the benefit of technology people cobble together a variety of jobs to eke out a living or supplement their earnings.

Throughout history, man has found ways to engage others in the work at hand to achieve greater goals. The classical theories of liberal economics reinforced and encouraged the division of labor and the freedom of exchanging work for pay without outside interference from the State or other influences. Tradesman guilds developed for the purpose of training and developing apprentices into masters in a specific craft were diminished when the work was divided into smaller pieces that an untrained worker could do (i.e., the division of labor). A series of unintended consequences resulted. Some of the means of engagement and goals, coupled with the power differential that accompanied financial means, resulted in employment exchanges that were often forced, undignified, dangerous, and unilaterally beneficial to the employer.

The employer had more than enough unskilled workers to replace those who either failed, were injured, or died on the job as workers flooded into urban centers for the plentiful work in the European Industrial Revolution.

> **Employers began to think of people, fellow human beings, as interchangeable parts in the economic machine; cogs in the proverbial wheel, if you will.**

Price, demand, and supply variables in the free market did nothing to counter the imbalance of power of employers over employees. The objectification of workers was made more manifest as demand greater than supply drove prices and profits up. The rich got richer and the poor got poorer.

Here we sit today with the same concern for rich over poor, exacerbated by the power and reach of social media. Technology has allowed for leveraging people all over the world for knowledge and services without the blessing of human interaction, mentoring, friendship, collegiality, or appreciation other than financial remuneration.

Too frequently, we business leaders lose sight of the mutual benefit of employer/employee relationships. Simon Sinek in his book, *Leaders Eat Last*, writes about how abstraction kills. The further we business leaders get from those doing the work, the more abstract these real human beings become and the more likely they will be subject to objectification by us; all passively condoned by the dominant ideology. Is it any surprise that workers sometimes fight against this abstraction and objectification with their feet, their voices, and their money?

Labor Unions

This topic will likely make some business leaders uncomfortable, but not for the reasons you think. The Church has and continues to speak into the fundamental rights of workers to protect themselves from unilaterally beneficial employment arrangements favoring employers. One of those fundamental human rights is the right to free and spontaneous association and the right for workers to organize. In *Rerum Novarum*, Pope Leo XIII reinforced the rights of workers to organize against abusive employers.:

> [48] . . . Among these may be enumerated societies for mutual help; various benevolent foundations established by private persons to provide for the workman, and for his widow or his orphans, in case of sudden calamity, in sickness, and in the event of death; and institutions for the welfare of boys and girls, young people, and those more advanced in years.

> [49] The most important of all are workingmen's unions, for these virtually include all the rest. History attests what excellent results were brought about the artificer's guilds of olden times. [. . .] We have spoken of them more than once, yet it will be well to explain here how notably they are needed, to show that they exist of their own right, and what should be their organization and their mode of action.

> [55] . . . They have taken up the cause of the working man, and have spared no efforts to better the condition both of families and individuals; to infuse a spirit of equity into the mutual relations of employers and employed; to keep before the eyes of both classes the precepts of duty and the laws of the Gospel – that

Gospel which, by inculcating self-restraint, keeps men within the bounds of moderation, and tends to establish harmony among the divergent interests and the various classes which compose the body politic. [. . .] We find therein grounds for the most cheering hope in the future, provided always that the associations we have described continue to grow and spread, and are well and wisely administered.

As recorded in the following excerpt, these labor organizations were implored to act consistent with the Church's teachings since the public institutions and the law had set aside the ancient religion.

> **The Church was trying to rightly reinstitute herself as the moral keel in society; the fixed set of moral laws, if you will; and expected these labor organizations to be a catalyst.**

[57] To sum up, then, we may lay it down as a general and lasting law that working mens' associations should be so organized and governed as to furnish the best and most suitable means for attaining what is aimed at, that is to say, for helping each individual member to better his condition to the utmost in body, soul, and property. It is clear that they must pay special and chief attention to the duties of religion and morality, and that social betterment should have this chiefly in view; otherwise they would lose wholly their special character, and end by becoming little better than those societies which take no account whatever of religion.

Pope Leo XIII encouraged labor unions to keep the Christian faith and morality at the forefront. Though protecting the right of workers to organize, he implored all men to that which is more natural: that capital (owner/employers) and labor (workers) be interdependent and respectful of one another.

> **If American business is going to return to truly mutually beneficial employer/employee exchanges business leaders must heed what Pope Leo labeled "The great mistake."**

> [19] The great mistake made in regard to the matter now under consideration (socialism) is to take up with the notion that class is naturally hostile to class, and that the wealthy and the working men are intended by nature to live in mutual conflict. **So irrational and so false is this view that the direct contrary is the truth.** Just as the symmetry of the human frame is the result of the suitable arrangement of the different parts of the body, so in a State is it ordained by nature that these two classes should dwell in harmony and agreement, so as to maintain the balance of the body politic. Each needs the other: capital cannot do without labor, nor labor without capital. *[Bold added for emphasis]*

Surprised?! Again, faith and reason reconcile here. Doesn't it make perfect sense that it is best that owners/employers and workers organize together not against one another?

For capital (employers) and labor (employees) to work together there exist specific and explicit responsibilities that each has to the other. Pope Leo XIII spelled these out in *Rerum Novarum*:

> [19] [. . .] First of all, there is no intermediary more powerful than religion (whereof the Church is the interpreter and guardian) in drawing the rich and the working class together, by reminding each of its duties to the other, and especially of the obligations of justice.

[20] Of these duties, the following bind the proletarian and the worker:

> Fully and faithfully to perform the work which has been freely and equitably agreed upon;
> never to injure the property, nor to outrage the person of an employer;
> never to resort to violence in defending their own cause;
> nor to engage in riot or disorder;
> and to have nothing to do with men of evil principles, who work upon the people with artful promises of great results and excite foolish hopes which usually end in useless regrets and grievous loss.

The following duties bind the wealthy owner and the employee:

> Not to look upon their work people as their bondsmen;
> But to respect in every man his dignity as a person ennobled by Christian character. They are reminded that, according to natural reason and Christian philosophy, working for gain is creditable, not shameful, to a man, since it enables him to earn an honorable livelihood; to misuse men as though they were things in the pursuit of gain, or to value them solely for their physical powers – that is truly shameful and inhuman.

Again, justice demands that, in dealing with the working man, religion and the good of his soul must be kept in mind. Hence the employer is bound:

> ➤ to see that the worker has time for his religious duties;
> ➤ that he not be exposed to corrupting influences and dangerous occasions;
> ➤ and that he be not led away to neglect his home and family, or to squander his earnings.
> ➤ Furthermore, the employer must never tax his work people beyond their strength,
> ➤ or employ them in work unsuited for their sex and age.

[. . .] but wealthy owners and masters of labor should be mindful of this – that to exercise pressure upon the indigent and the destitute for the sake of gain, and to gather one's profit out of the need of another, is condemned by all laws, human and divine.

[21] But the Church, with Jesus Christ as her Master and Guide, aims **higher still**. She lays down precepts yet more perfect and tries to bind class to class in friendliness and good feeling. *[Bold added for emphasis]*

Is it not true that a business enterprise organized together is more likely to achieve its given mission than an enterprise where resources and energy are wasted fighting within? I would argue even more directly that it is impossible to optimize enterprise results with labor organizing against management. I've worked and led in both environments and my experience significantly informs this assertion. This perspective is offered not in contrast to the rights of workers to organize, but simply to draw attention to the responsibilities of owners/employers to do at least as much for workers as labor unions expect to do.

Note also that the diminishing presence of and respect for the Christian faith and the Church has likely done great damage to the normative employer/employee relationship in modern times.

Without the moral keel of the Church, how true is it that the human worker is often objectified and treated as expendable in the pursuit of profit? Setting aside the ancient religion has had dire and devastating effects on the actions of man, employers and employees alike.

Those of you who think these century-old thoughts on labor unions are outdated might consider the caution Saint John Paul II wrote about in his Papal Encyclical, *Laborem Exercens*, in 1981: The error of earlier capitalism can be repeated wherever man is in a way treated on the same level as the whole complex of the material means of production, as an instrument and not in accordance with the true dignity of his work.[166]

> Saint John Paul II further described an organizing reaction (of labor) in response to a system of injustice and harm; so much so that it "cried out to heaven for vengeance."[167]

Even in 1981, Saint John Paul II called for new movements of solidarity of workers, and note this, **with** workers.[168] He uses the term "economism" to describe a fundamental error; a term that considers human labor solely according to its economic purpose. Man should be served by the means of business, not be used as a means therein.[169] He further explains, "The attainment of worker's rights cannot, however, be doomed to be merely a result of economic systems which on a larger or smaller scale are guided chiefly by the criterion of maximum profit."[170]

Catholic Social Teaching does not hold that unions are no more than a reflection of the "class" structure of society and that they are a mouthpiece for a class struggle which inevitably governs social life. They are indeed a mouthpiece for the struggle for social justice. This struggle should be seen as a normal endeavor "for" the just good; it is not a struggle "against" others.[171] Wow. Truth.

Today, with the advent of technology and the growth of social media, organic and spontaneous forms of organizing are taking shape.

The ability of one person to be heard around the world in mere seconds, has significantly shifted the power differential from employers to employees. Most millennials won't hesitate to post and bring attention to abusive power, stirring the pot of unrest. The millennial trust wick is so short due to their media-influenced opinions of business, that they often begin work with a chip on their shoulder. Their tender egos developed after years of helicopter parenting and ribbons and trophies for everyone has not prepared them well for the harshness of reality where performance really matters. Their tenderness and lack of trust are a recipe for early exits from employers with lots of e-fanfare. A general lack of leadership in millennials and engrained individualism, yet no lack of personal passion, will likely change the nature of spontaneous organizing, but the rights and related outcomes won't change. Workers will fight against corrupt and/or abusive power, and you can bet millennials will be leading the charge!

The core issue of recognizing the dignity of human beings at work is now lost in the two-way pollution of what could be and should be a free and mutually beneficial exchange. Worse yet, both employers and employees too often accept it as 'just the way it is.'

> **The bargaining unit and mediated negotiations of today are now part of the institutionalized polluted free market for talent, versus what-should-be-mutually beneficial exchange of work for pay.**

The baby (free markets or capitalism) was tossed out with the bath water of abusiveness. Attempts to remedy untenable employer/employee relations are now tempered and governed by bureaucrats who, with all good intentions, concern themselves with compliance and preservation of self. Others-centeredness is a vague abstraction from the original nature of business and the good that is meant to be inherent in employer/employee exchanges; save the pre-requisite of virtue, excellent leadership, optimized cooperation, and increased value creation. How far we've fallen and how clouded is the truth of business by the institution of business?!

Use of Excess Capital for Job Creation

Mutually beneficial employment relationships are not the only casualty of a virtue-starved marketplace. Virtuous leadership can also impact how capital generated from profit or "justice earned"[172] can be used to make a greater impact on the common good and society. Before we dive into this topic, remember the marker we left earlier in this book for those whose earnings did not allow them to participate in mutually beneficial exchanges, pushing them toward the margin of society? This part of the book is theirs.

Individual philanthropy and generous giving to not-for-profit enterprises is a current medium by which distributed business wealth is used to benefit many who are marginalized in society. This financial help has been and is essential. You might categorize this type of giving as relief and betterment. Notwithstanding this benefit, is it possible that wealth retained in a business for the explicit purpose of job creation might provide an even greater social benefit? Some scholars suggest that profits or capital retained or re-invested to create more wealth is tainted with the stain of self-interest.[173]

This belief would indicate that the more capital re-invested in business means less philanthropic giving. Does this hold true, even if financial returns on subsequent investments render no financial returns? Regardless of the impact on philanthropic giving, ask yourself, "Which provides more value to society and to the common good?"

In his Encyclical Letter, *Quadragesimo Anno*, written in May 1931, Pope Pius XI shared this thought, "Expending larger incomes so that opportunity for gainful work may be abundant, provided, however, that this work is applied to producing really useful goods, ought to be considered, as we deduce from the principles of the Angelic Doctor, an outstanding exemplification of the virtue of munificence (great generosity) and one particularly suited to the needs of the times."[174]

Note the times are in the midst of the Great Depression. Creating gainful work that produces really useful goods, and the availability of employment and its suitability for the times are both significant themes in this thought. I would suggest both are relevant today and business leaders are uniquely positioned and gifted to provide gainful employment. Gainful employment should not be arbitrary or meaningless and entrepreneurship or intrepreneurship can provide the scope and boundaries of utility for the goods or services to be produced, ensuring work's rightful application.

Church charity or missions trends are leaning in the direction of less philanthropy and more sustainable and transformational answers to some to the world's biggest and long-lasting problems.

> **People with resources are generally tired of writing ever-increasing check amounts each year with little-to-no gain against the core problems in society, here or abroad.**

This type of munificence is not sustainable against a backdrop of ever-increasing needs of those marginalized in society. In addition, giving of alms and providing for others what they could provide for themselves violates respect for their dignity and creates unhealthy dependencies. Sure, meeting acute and emergent needs is essential and required at times; relief and betterment if you will; but continuing giving and support beyond that which is required creates circumstances where those originally benefiting are actually worse off than before they had the need.[175]

Couple the business leaders' unique capability for creativity, innovation, access to markets of exchange, and capital resources generated through the operation of a healthy business with those needs of society and we've got a divine alignment that can make great gains against some of the world's biggest problems! But some business paradigms and beliefs must change to make this transition to dignified and philanthropic job creation a reality.

The first of these business paradigms to change is an expectation of a quick return on capital invested. The term "patient capital" is used to represent this paradigm shift. As business leaders and philanthropists begin to engage in creating sustainable and transformative solutions, they are often faced with no financial returns in the foreseeable future and economic returns that only hint at positive financial returns in the long-term with no guarantees. If the philanthropist views his or her investment through a lens that expects normal magnitude and timing of capital returns, the effort will be abandoned in short order. But if the business leader/philanthropist views their investment through the lens of human dignity, the common good, patient capital, and shrinking negative returns in the absence of positive returns, then this alternative "giving" strategy has real potential.

Allow me to illustrate the logic of patient capital vs. the giving of alms. When one gives generously to a philanthropy or charity, they do so understanding that good work will be done to meet immediate and acute needs of those warranting service from the non-profit enterprise. Generous giving expectations are met. What most who give in this way understand is that they will likely get a call or card next year, asking for a similar or greater gift. The financial return on their investment is zero resulting in a 100% loss of their gift, corpus, or investment, though undoubtedly some qualitative good came from their generosity. How much better might this giving relationship or transaction be if the business leader/philanthropist would only lose 75% of his or her gift, corpus, or investment, requiring less capital investment and the potential of less loss of their recurring investment in future years. This would allow the business leader/philanthropist to redirect some of their philanthropic and charitable investment to other causes or allow their beneficiary to redeploy resources in other more economically sustainable ways and growth.

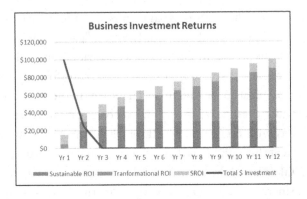

Here is a graph of a typical business investment return expectation: significant investment up front with returns expected in a 2 to 3-year time frame. Of course, the timing and magnitude of the return will vary based upon the nature of the business and related risk. The sustainable ROI represents what would be considered traditional financial return on a capital investment. Transformational ROI represents the impact of a business on the lives of those touched by it through compensation, quality of life, skills enhancement, and self-efficacy. The Social ROI (SROI) represents the benefits to the greater community and society.

Here is a similar graph showing what the sustainable return is on a typical charitable donation/investment for the same 12 consecutive years:

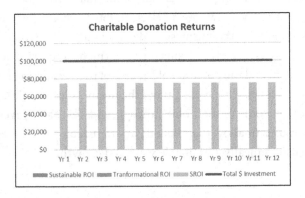

The SROI is the good relief and betterment can do, but note there is no sustainable or transformational ROI! Notice, though, the SROI is only achieved when the same investment is made each year! The question is, "Can a reoriented investment from businesspeople create a greater return over the same time frame that solves core problems that manifest in some of society's biggest problems?"

Let's look at what a $100,000 investment can do if invested in sustainable and transformational ways:

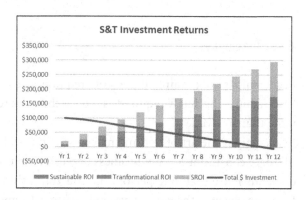

This investment can come from increased employment of those hard to employ, investing in ways to deliver groceries in a food desert, providing seed money for urban entrepreneurs, and number of ways a business can invest some of its wealth for the common good and to dignify those who might receive the benefits from business. Notice a sustainable and transformational (S&T) investment generates a triple return like a business does with a stronger social return on investment (SROI), but also provides reduced future investments (not true for charitable contributions) providing lower investments in the future or the ability to redirect investments to other pressing needs.

This is exactly what can happen when Christian business leaders use their excess capital generated; not as individual philanthropy or charitable contributions originating from distributed wealth but retain it for the purpose of meaningful job creation, even though specific financial returns might be long-in-coming. The return on this type of investment is significantly greater-than zero and the percentage loss of investment is significantly less.

Imagine if this idea for using excess capital became part of the purpose of and culture of your business today. Might this interest your employees, suppliers, community, and even your shareholders? Business success like this respects the human dignity of others, serves the common good, and allows others to flourish at work – all part of a transcendent business.

Chapter 6 Key Takeaways

1. Leadership is not required if the work requires just you.
2. Leadership is absolutely required as soon as the work requires more than just you.
3. Leadership is the art of optimizing cooperation, and it's the ultimate constraint for any business because once the work demands more than one person, the constraint shifts away from the object of the work to your ability to get someone to cooperate with you in the work at hand.
4. This definition has Biblical roots in Ecclesiastes 4:9 (NIV) "Two are better than one because they have good return for their work."
5. It makes sense that other people tend to cooperate more when their leader is virtuous: wise, just, temperate, and courageous, yielding the ultimate competitive advantage in an enterprise's people and their commitment to the work.
6. The enhanced competitive advantage in a free market delivers more value creation, more wealth, which demands more virtue to stay the course.
7. The economic cycle spirals upward when we business leaders practice virtue and reorient business' purpose toward human flourishing and transcendence.
8. The Church supports the rights of workers to organize, while condemning the idea that owners/employers (capital) and workers/employees (labor) should organize against one another. They refer to this notion as the "Great Mistake."

9. There are significant physical, economic, and spiritual responsibilities that capital and labor owe to one another, but absent the influence of the Church and the Christian faith, those responsibilities have been clouded by the institution of business.

10. Capital retained in business for the purpose of creating jobs and protecting the dignity of others may well be a better and more effective use of wealth deployed to serve those in need.

11. The idea of patient capital invested to solve some of the world's biggest problems is gaining ground against traditional philanthropic giving that leaves core problems unsolved and are sustained only by perpetual and increased giving over time.

12. Reordering what businesses do with their increased wealth generated from improved value creation due to the enhanced cooperation between employers and employees is part of reorienting business toward its transcendence purpose, a true force for God, not just for good.

Chapter 6 Synopsis

Competitive advantage once attained, is hard to sustain in today's competitive marketplace. The ultimate competitive advantage is a business leader's ability to get others to cooperate fully and willingly in the work at hand. Why? Because getting others to cooperate or help you is the ultimate constraint in any business. This poses significant implications on what business leaders do and the purpose thereof. Furthermore, this reorientation of business toward human flourishing and transcendence demands that management and labor organize together, and that accumulated wealth be used in ways that foster human dignity and pursue the common good.

CHAPTER 7

Virtuosos

~ତ୍ତ୍ର

WE EXPECT THAT SOME of you, while excited about the possibilities and precepts offered in the previous chapters of this book, are skeptical about the real probability of success as measured by any traditional business metric; not the least of which are revenue growth, net profit, employee retention, customer loyalty, supplier loyalty, and overall competitiveness. Anticipating this skepticism in 2013, we (several talented student researchers and I) sought out and began to study companies that have excelled in the U.S. free market and in their respective industries while practicing virtue (evidencing a fixed set of moral rules). We call these companies, and specifically their leaders, Virtuosos.

It's likely you'll be shocked at not only their results, but at the creativity with which they authorized, expected, and implemented virtue into the practice of their business. In all cases, none of these business leaders sought us out. We sought them out. There's wisdom here we want to share, and it is a premise on which we continue to operate and research. You will find this wisdom in *The Holy Bible* (NIV), Proverbs 27:2, "Let another praise you, and not your own mouth; someone else, and not your own lips." It has been an incredible privilege to spend time in these companies, ask probing questions, and bear witness to the benefits of virtue and free markets. We take the trust and access offered us seriously and commit to you to provide honest and thorough reflections of each Virtuoso leader and company. We humbly accept the role of "another" here.

As you read these real cases, you will find decisions made that perhaps you'd simply make out of business acumen or competence. There is remarkable consistency between the actions of virtuous business leaders and progressive, people-centered management practices. But beware! In the book *The Anatomy of Peace* by The Arbinger Institute, the authors share the premise that there is something deeper than behavior: one's way of being. I suggest one's way of being is better defined by what one believes and values about people. Do you believe a business leader should treat people as people or people as objects? Your motivation for doing what you do makes a critical difference to your people. You can be duplicitous only for a short time before your way of being is revealed. It's the constancy and consistency, girded by virtue, that makes these creative and successful companies Virtuosos.

You'll find in each story a brief history of the Virtuoso company and its business leader(s), a summary of the underlying values and beliefs that define the uniqueness of the company, numerous business practices in which these values and beliefs are manifested, and closing thoughts that help tie the Virtuosos back to the tenets of this book. At the end of the day, we hope you find some models and practices that may inform your pursuit of a transcendent business. Certainly, filtering for preferences and consolidating some practices to make them your own is invited and encouraged. We invite collaboration of the highest order!

Enjoy reading these stories of those who have gone before you. May their experience bless your journey toward truth and a transcendent business.

The Most Human Company
The Onyx Collection
Belvue, Kansas

If you were to sneeze, you'd likely miss Belvue, Kansas, located on Highway 24 between Topeka and Manhattan, Kansas. This is true except for the cars overflowing out of a parking lot threatening to overtake the highway in front of a very nondescript building on the east end of town. At second glance at dusk or after dark, your eyes might be drawn to something brightly lit just outside the employee entrance of the company; a brick-and-mortar memorial or grotto to the Blessed Mother Mary. This is the home and world headquarters of The Onyx Collection (Onyx).

This tiny-Kansas-town company employs almost 600 people and produces 50-plus tons of product a day. Their product: cast shower bases, shower walls, and accessories. Ninety-five percent of the product produced any given day will be shipped the next day to customers. Quality "guaranteed for life," little-to-no work-in-process, a loyal and growing customer base, and competitors who can't make it or do it any better is a great formula for success. As a matter of fact, many of Onyx's current customers used to be their competitors. In the market stumbles of 2001 and 2008, competing companies were not able to continue their manufacturing operations and remain viable. Though still installing bathroom vanities and showers, they turned to The Onyx Collection to provide quality, on-time service of vanity tops and shower bases and walls at affordable prices. Why they did this is a story of lore, if it were only untrue.

With annual sales exceeding $100 million and its growing trucking/transportation company, Onyx has grown through the individual contributions of all its employees; even those hired back in 1985 when the company started. Yes, really. Former U.S. Congressional Representative from Kansas, Lynn Jenkins, made a visit to Onyx in the mid-2010's. Her comment thereafter was, "This is the most human company I have ever seen." Onyx is a shining example of how a reluctant leader learns and listens to others to build a transcendent business that is an industry leader; all the while remaining true to his faith and the virtues that accompany his effort as CEO, citizen, individual, husband, father, and grandfather. You'd find it hard to identify the CEO of Onyx wandering the building. No corner office. In fact, no office at all! He has a standing workstation amidst numerous other workers in the office area of the headquarters. Meet Bob Awerkamp.

Company History

Bob Awerkamp grew up working with his hands as a machinist and tool and die maker in Quincy, Illinois. As he recollects, anyone in that business, especially in the Midwest, is keenly aware of the urgency and quality demanded to fix any broken piece of farm equipment, a stranded river barge, or a damaged swing bridge across the Mississippi River. No high-quality and urgent fix means no business, no revenue, and no food on the table. Concern for quality and service were forged in Bob during these times and in that role.

Bob earned a bachelor's degree from Quincy College (now University) where its Franciscan roots and influence inspired the set of values and beliefs that he carries with him today. In 1963, Bob entered the U.S. Navy and quickly earned the respect of veteran soldiers and his Admiral's staff through his practical quality and service orientation to solving problems. At age 40, Bob relocated to St. Marys, Kansas and began working and selling for a cabinet-making shop. It was in this role that he stumbled across a cast vanity top maker who wanted out of the business. He listened to his pitch but declined. "What's a machinist know about making cast vanity tops?"

But something kept gnawing at him. In his hometown of St. Marys, he kept witnessing teenager after teenager leaving the small town for the shiny promise of the bigger cities where they could chase their worldly dreams; only to return broke, unemployed, with a family on the rocks, and wondering what happened. Bob recalls with a smile,

"They were trading a scapular for a new pickup truck and gold chain around their neck."

Bob tried to talk his friends and colleagues to take on the cast vanity top business with the goal of keeping the town's young adults in or near St. Marys, in a healthy community where their faith and related values would form them into faithful and productive individuals, citizens, and spouses. There were no takers. Back then Bob recalls that anyone could cast a vanity top in their garage! He'd lament, "What good is a commodity business with few or no barriers to entry?!" Yet the problem of the town's young people continued to manifest in his holy discontent and would not wane.

Finally, and reluctantly in the mid-1980's, Bob learned the cast vanity business in a garage in Junction City, Kansas. With his problem-solving and entrepreneurial mind active, he saw the cast vanity top opportunity as a way to meet a market need and, more importantly, as a salve to remedy the problem of quick-adventuring young people leaving St. Marys. He could offer these young people competitive wages, salaries, and benefits, and coach them appropriately in responsible living. In 1985, he started The Onyx Collection, named after the translucent mineral that gives many vanity tops their unique quartz-like appearance.

Underlying Values and Beliefs

The things we learn and value as business leaders become the cornerstones of the culture and values of our businesses if we are integral leaders thereof. Bob Awerkamp and Onyx are a shining example of this phenomenon. Following are a series of values lived by the leaders in the company that define how Onyx brings employees together to compete well in their industry. The cardinal virtues most closely correlated to the specific value or belief clarified are shared in brackets.

Free markets must prevail. Ultimately, free markets create more value for all and, with the right set of underlying beliefs, a company can create wealth for many; can create improvements in one's community; and can convert cutthroat competition into raving fans cooperating to serve the market better. Accordingly, one should not seek to monopolize or corner the market. Exclusive territories run contrary to this thinking. Don't place boundaries around sales territories. Exclusivity, counter-intuitively creates a competitive vs. a cooperative environment. Because exclusivity is unnatural, people are compelled to seek to overthrow someone who has a kingdom or monopoly. Let the best win and invite others to do better. In this way, value is an ever-increasing proposition. [prudence, justice]

Partnerships don't work. Decisions are not made by committee. Individuals make decisions. Bob has not known any partnerships to survive the pressures of the marketplace, though, there may be a few. Being beholden to another causes discounting, if not diminishing of values aimed toward ends that may differ under pressure. If constancy of purpose and consistency of values are to be maintained, a singular leader is best. [prudence]

Bob has allowed family members into the business. Two of his sons and one of his daughters are now owners, leaders, and active in it. When asked about the potential difficulties that often accompany nepotism, Bob responded that problems with nepotism can be mitigated if two things exist: absolute alignment of values (as in no partnership), and the absolute competence of family members that garners respect from others. [prudence, courage]

Seven years of harvest; seven years of famine. Biblically instructive, businesses go through peaks and troughs of prosperity. To survive the troughs, businesses must store up reserves during the years of plenty. Onyx does this and by doing so has not only survived troughs, but has become the supplier of choice as competitors who did not store up reserves had to abandon the business. By the way, Onyx never stopped production during the 2020 COVID-19 Pandemic either. [prudence, temperance]

No teams. Each individual is important and each brings a unique set of gifts, skills, talents, and learned capabilities to an enterprise. In practice, the integration of roles across multiple functions supported by common goals and aligned compensation practices yields results normally thought to accompany teams. Bob prefers to think of the entire company as "the team" and every individual deserves to be recognized and honored for who he or she is with no intermediary associated with a secondary team designation. This may be less possible with size and scale. [prudence, justice]

Adopt technology early. In a free market, innovation and technologies will constantly be introduced. Embrace the changes; not at the expense of labor or jobs, but to create economies of scale that allow growth while maintaining or reducing costs. Onyx's software is developed and maintained in-house allowing them to control the pace of IT innovation. [prudence]

Share knowledge. This value, surprisingly, applies both inside the company and with those outside the company. Innovations are not intended to create singular competitive advantages, but they are intended to enhance an entire industry and create more value for all. Onyx has both lent vanity top molds to competitors and borrowed them. The company offers tours to anyone and everyone (including our team) and this includes their competitors! Yes, this sounds extremely counter-cultural given current business ideologies, yet Onyx has been the ultimate benefactor of exchanging innovations freely as the respect gained for doing so has earned business from competitors during industry troughs. [prudence, courage]

Own vs. lease equipment. Owning capital equipment requires retained profit. Retaining enough cash to buy capital equipment requires subordinating one's personal interest (by drawing cash out of the business) to the preference for cash required to grow the enterprise. Growth is also required to support the negative impact on cash flow of buying capital equipment while financing ever-growing receivables. This particular value, without growth, is unsustainable in the long term. [prudence, temperance, courage]

No marketing. This sounds odd, especially for an industry leader! Onyx's website is informational in nature, but it is not self-promoting. Bob believes that word-of-mouth is the best form of marketing and execution (delivering on one's promise) is the best way to ensure word-of-mouth marketing. And, yes, Onyx has experienced double-digit growth and more for decades with no self-promotion. Marketing causes people to buy what they don't need. Sharing this belief did not come without a chuckle from Bob reflecting on his stumble into business as a salesman for a cabinet-making company. [prudence, courage, temperance]

Stand on principle. Standing on principle may not win you any friends, but it will earn you the right friends and you'll know who your friends are. In practice, standing on principle is critical to the alignment of values. Those who don't like principle can leave the company. Those who share belief in the principle can and will stay a long time. [prudence, courage]

Leadership accrues to those willing to accept the responsibility for it. Given titles and promotions expose others to the disgrace of public failure if they fail to perform as designated leaders. Those who voluntarily step into a void of leadership, having the competency and character to fix problems and inspire others to greater things are, conversely, subjected to grace and mercy. [prudence, justice]

Business Practices

In any business, values are only as influential as they are manifested in business practices. What follows is an inexhaustive list of how Onyx's values are manifested in some of their company practices. Cardinal virtues and relevant Catholic Social Teaching principles are shared in brackets.

Recruiting and hiring. Hiring decisions are made by those accepting responsibility for leadership. [subsidiarity] The Onyx Collection's application for employment consists of four categories/questions and must be completed by hand, in person. The four questions are EDUCATION (include any non-credit courses taken – showing initiative to learn); JOB EXPERIENCE (be specific about what you've done); ACCOMPLISHMENTS (done on your own initiative); INTERESTS & HOBBIES (what you do in your spare time).

Communication. Almost all of the workstations in the factory and office are standing workstations. This encourages movement, energy, spontaneous interaction (if one is already on their feet, then going to ask someone else a question is an easy natural extension), and cooperation. Sitting encourages e-mail communication, phone calls, or worse yet, no communication at all.

Employee compensation and benefits. Employees are paid current, meaning on Friday they are paid through Wednesday of the same week. The only lag is the administrative time to accurately process payroll for almost 600 employees. This practice gets employees paid quickly for the work performed and invested in the company. Onyx acts consistently with Deuteronomy 24:14-15 (*The Holy Bible -RSV*) by doing their best to not withhold past sundown a man's wage.[176]

Bonus or gain-sharing pools are earned through a combination of company attendance, throughput, and orders. One's level of participation can increase weekly based upon gained/shared knowledge, acceptance of more responsibility, and overall work performance. Weekly, those accepting responsibility for leadership assess those with whom they work and adjust participation levels consistent with work performance. To pull this off, those accepting responsibility must be and remain very close to the work and the workers. When we toured Onyx, those accepting responsibility for leadership were not readily identifiable from those who had not. [justice, human dignity]

Onyx pays 100% of the healthcare insurance premiums for employees and their families. For all practical purposes, they are self-insured, except for insurance to cover catastrophic illnesses or injuries for which the company also pays the entire insurance premium. [justice, temperance]

Executive compensation. Tax laws and exposure to potential questions dictate that executives take a significant salary for covering their personal tax liability. But the Onyx executives often reinvest any excess back into the company. When asked several years ago about how he handled his wealth generated from owning a $50-million manufacturing enterprise, Bob responded, "I don't know if I've ever had wealth." He shared with us that he just put central heat into the home he has lived in for over 30 years. [temperance]

Serving customers. All employees have the freedom and blessing to serve customers in any way that makes sense. Stories of heroic customer recovery actions are prevalent and, admittedly, have been the basis for customer growth in new regions of the country. Onyx has been known to ship a single vanity top, dead head (with no freight coming back), across the country to meet an installer's deadline. [justice, temperance]

Integration of faith allowed and encouraged. Many of the faith-specific practices shared at Onyx are employee initiated. At the request of an employee, the company was consecrated to the Sacred Heart of Jesus in 1997. In 2002, at the request of another employee, the company was further consecrated to the Virgin Mary; evidenced by the bricks-and-mortar memorial to the Virgin Mary brightly lit just outside the employee entrance. Employees are allowed to adorn their work areas with hand-made crucifixes or other relics evidencing their confidence in their faith. [courage]

Daily prayer at different locations throughout the company factory and headquarters is initiated and led by employees. The company chooses to close its doors on all Catholic Holy Days so all employees can tend to that which is most important: God, family, and community. Since the founding of Onyx, several other businesses in the area do the same. [courage]

Closing Thoughts

So, what's the key to Onyx's success? It is certainly not the ripe and early-entry market with foreseeable competitive advantage from the outset. Is it the unique talent found in rural Kansas? The Silicon Valley-gone-rogue minds between Topeka and Manhattan, Kansas? Is it the unique technologies deployed and protected as intellectual property? Is it the front man; the dynamic public figure that is the darling of investors and the public relations machine? Hardly.

One of your serious considerations of the cause for success should be the alignment of business practices to core values and beliefs, embraced from the top to the bottom of the enterprise. This type of alignment is coached in any strategic leadership book worth its salt. Is this the "genie" or secret sauce? It certainly is contributory to success. But might there be something more about this "most human company?"

How contrary are some of the business practices (evidencing the company's values and beliefs) at Onyx to those more aligned with the dominate ideology of the purpose of business; to maximize shareholder wealth? While likely unsettling to many because they are so different, it is hard to deny that the alignment of business practices with beliefs, values, and virtues consistent with our human nature yields a successful and results-oriented business that is hard to compete against and even more difficult to emulate. Perhaps Onyx is even a transcendent business in which people are loved, cared for, and allowed to flourish on all fronts; not the least of which is spiritually.

Gary Hamel, best-selling author and educator, shared in his book *The Future of Management*, that a new management model is far more advantageous to a business than any specific strategic competitive advantage.[177] The Onyx Collection is certainly manifest evidence of that.

Serving Those in Need
Tim Haahs Engineers and Architects
Blue Bell, Pennsylvania

"I will give you a new heart and put a new spirit within you; I will remove from you your heart of stone and give you a heart of flesh." – The Holy Bible (NIV), Ezekiel 36:26[178]

Tim Haahs is a man with a big heart. In fact, it's a relatively new heart; his third physical heart within his brief 60+ years on this earth. Tim has been described by others as a man with great ambition and passion, as one would expect of someone who has achieved as much as Tim has. Yet his greatest achievements often go unnoticed. Certainly, his descent into greatness is a story for the ages.

At the relatively young age of 33 and thriving within the ranks of a prevailing engineering and architecture firm in Philadelphia specializing in designing and engineering parking structures, Tim was invited to join the group of principles/owners of the firm; an achievement few at that age earn without sacrificing time and energy doing other things. Shortly thereafter, the world as he knew it changed drastically and his future that was so bright became like a fading ember of a candle wick abruptly extinguished.

One day while driving down the New Jersey turnpike, Tim awoke to find his car in the middle of the highway, stopped, and running with little-to-no recollection of what happened or why he was there. He had collapsed while driving. Tim managed to make it home, but as his condition worsened, a friend transported him to the hospital for diagnosis. To everyone's surprise, the doctors diagnosed a serious and previously unidentified heart ailment that would require a heart transplant if Tim was to have a future. Tim was relegated from his recently earned corner office to a cardiac ward hospital room waiting for a heart transplant. It is in places like this where those so relegated are forced to face their own mortality and the value of their life to date. Tim did so. During his walk-back and walk-through, Tim asked God to not just heal his heart, but to heal him as a person. Bargaining as many might in these mortal circumstances, Tim promised, if so rewarded, that he would serve God fully with the balance of his life. And so began the path forthwith told.

After six months of waiting, hundreds of thousands of dollars of medical bills, and near death, Tim was granted a second chance with a transplanted heart. In the process, he had exhausted his health insurance benefits and was forced to rely on the generosity and good will of family, friends, and the charity of the hospital and doctors who were treating him, a huge serving of humble pie for such a young, successful, and independent businessperson. During recovery, having recalled his promise to God, Tim began his life's dedication to God and toward helping others in need, mirroring those who had helped him in his time of need.

As hope for a future grew, Tim expected to be able to start back where he left off at the company that promoted him, but he found out after returning that the culture of the firm, while not bad, simply would not allow him to pursue that which was most important to him now – serving those in need. He had to choose between pursuits that dominated him prior to his incident and new life where he could fulfill his promise to God. Tim decided to leave and start his own firm. With a computer purchased by his brother – because there was no money after all the anti-rejection drugs had been purchased and the hospital bills remained unpaid – Timothy Haahs and Associates was born.

Company History

Timothy Haahs and Associates was officially incorporated in March 1994 and operated out of the family's garage. Committed to flourishing in his own business, during a visit to his cardiologist for a regular check-up, Tim shared that he had started his own parking structure design and engineering firm and asked if there were any projects at the hospital on which he and his small team could work.

The extraordinary kindness Tim showed as a patient in the cardiac unit while waiting for his transplant accrued to him in grace and favor when looking for work. His request resulted in two hospital parking structure projects accruing to the benefit of his newly created firm. They were in business!

Though small and running on very little capital, the company grew at a steady pace. After two years of operating out of the garage, the company moved to a new office outside his home to help absorb the growth. Tim Haahs and Associates had already begun operating under its new mission to help those in need. At about the same time, Tim and an associate, started Calvary Vision Church, a non-denominational Christian church. At the urging of people he respected, Tim was asked to be Pastor of the fledgling church. With no formal seminary training, Tim first balked at the idea, but with a leap of faith, Tim agreed to serve the church and enrolled in seminary.

With the future looking up, fate dealt Tim another blow that both challenged and forged his faith. The heart transplant performed in 1993 before starting his own firm was done expeditiously to keep Tim alive, but the heart was not ideal. That less-than-ideal heart began to fail. Tim found himself back in the cardiac unit waiting for another heart transplant.

While in the hospital, Tim continued to be engaged in his business, led the firm, worshipped with his congregation (yes, in the cardiac unit), and impacted the lives of those around him in the hospital. His others-centeredness ultimately manifested in Tim, next on the transplant list, passing on an available heart for the sake of another cardiac transplant patient closer to death than he was; trusting God would provide. His trust was well-placed and a brief wait he received a new, healthy heart; the heart that beats in his chest to this day. Tim's promise to serve those in need was alive and well, and he set forth again to do just that.

Steady and aggressive growth followed the firm's efforts. In the early 2000's, the firm grew to a regional presence with offices in New Brunswick, New Jersey; Miami, Florida; and Atlanta, Georgia. The growth demanded a new location which would serve both the company and the church better. In 2001, Tim moved his firm and his church to the building in which they currently reside in Blue Bell, Pennsylvania. Yes, the same building. In the building, one door to Tim's office opens to his firm while the other opens to Calvary Vision Church. The firm employs over 50 professionals spread across their four offices and generates between $7 and $9 million in annual project revenue.

Tim as the CEO and Founder, and the firm as a whole, have received dozens of top business awards since the late 1990's. Tim won Ernst & Young Entrepreneur of the Year in 1998 in the Philadelphia region. In 2016, Tim received the Ellis Island Medal of Honor. Tim Haahs and Associates has been recognized many years in succession as one of the top places to work and as one of the fastest growing small companies in the Philadelphia region. Their parking structure and mixed-use projects have won numerous design awards. In 2012, Tim was appointed by the Obama Administration and confirmed by the U.S. Senate to the National Institute of Building Sciences in Washington, D.C.

Consistent with their mission to help those in need, the firm prioritizes building projects for hospitals, schools, and other charitable and social institutions that have a focus on helping others. Not only does Tim expect high quality work and service to be provided to their clients, but he also wants their project to have a lasting, positive impact on the people and community around them. Yes, through parking structures!

Underlying Values and Beliefs

Tim knew that to fulfill the firm's mission of helping those in need that he had to develop a mission statement and core values that could guide his firm's everyday operating philosophy and related decisions. We share those core beliefs and values in the pages that follow. In brackets are the cardinal virtues most clearly correlated to the specific value or belief shared.

Mission and vision clarity. The Timothy Haahs and Associates Mission Statement is:

➢ **We exist** to help those in need. [justice]
➢ **We emphasize** assisting those medical, religious, and charitable organizations (as well as individuals) directly involved with helping those who are in need. [justice]
➢ **We believe** that the best way to accomplish this mission is to become a recognized leader in our chosen field and profession, and to provide engineering and architectural services that are not merely adequate, but distinguished. [prudence]
➢ **We will** use to the best of our abilities, our God-given talents in architectural design, structural engineering, parking consultation, and project management. [prudence]

Tim Haahs acknowledges and embraces the risk of accountability that comes with a mission like this. Without an overwhelming commitment to it, this kind of mission can easily appear to be a gimmick or the shadow of a true contrary mission and can backfire on the company.

Avoid the bread of idleness. The firm expects a significant commitment of time from all employees to deliver on its service promise to clients; on its mission promise to those within the company; and on its promise to those in need who might benefit from their work and resources. A significant work ethic is expected of everyone. Unlike many people, Tim chose a lifetime of no guarantees of income over a lifetime of disability benefits funded by the American taxpayer. He walks the walk.

Speak life into core values. Tim Haahs and Associates has three core values that are clearly stated. They are:

➢ Go the extra mile
➢ Return all calls the same day
➢ Keep clients and the staff informed

Translating core values into actionable steps is a key for clarity and execution. Going the extra mile is translated as simply helping another person beyond reason and rationale. Walking the walk again, Tim had the courage and humility to go door-to-door and ask for excess medications from other heart transplant survivors when he couldn't afford his post-transplant medications. He expects his employees to practice the same courage and humility to help someone else as a client, as a fellow employee, or as someone in need. [courage, temperance]

The second core value emphasizes that all employees return all calls the same day. No translation needed. With technical professionals, communication is not often a strong suit. This, Tim believes, is not only important for communication, but also critical for building relationships; another competence not found generously in engineering and architecture professionals. [prudence]

Finally, the third core value is literal as well. Again, this value helps build trust in relationships with coworkers and clients and builds teamwork amongst those in the firm, vendors, and clients. [prudence]

Build relationships. Tim looks at business development through the lens of relationship-building; a practice not unique to most businesses. But Tim uses the story of his life, work, and God's hand therein as a hard-to-forget memory. Even after 10, 15, or 20 years, those hearing his story might be in a position to make organizational decisions, and if those decisions involve parking or parking structures, perhaps they'll remember Tim Haahs and Associates. Like Tim, when you place yourself in situations where God is needed, or God places you in extraordinarily difficult circumstances giving Him room to work, you create the opportunity to tell His story and honor God in the process.

Build trust – At Tim Haahs & Associates, trust is definitely earned. Tim makes most decisions until one shows the ability to filter decision criteria consistent with the mission and values of the firm. Once earned, though, trust is poured on others. Those who commit fully to the mission of the firm will receive more. *The Holy Bible* (NIV) in Luke 16:10 records, "Whoever can be trusted with very little can also be trusted with much, and whoever is dishonest with very little will also be dishonest with much."[179] [justice, courage]

Lead and make decisions. Decisions at Tim Haahs and Associates are not made by consensus. When any type of decision must be made, Tim believes that there must be someone to make the call and be held accountable for the overall decision. Tim does not shy away from this responsibility and has embraced it on numerous occasions. However, being the final decision maker does not mean that he does not seek and receive counsel from his Board of Directors, the executive staff, and/or others in the firm. In reality, the firm is not required to have a Board, but he chooses to have one so that he can get advice and support from others with wisdom and expertise. In every organization, there must be someone with whom the "buck stops" as the phrase goes. At Tim Haahs & Associates, that is at Tim's desk.

View individuals holistically and pray for them. Tim Haahs has been known to reach others by stepping beyond his normal and expected duties as President/CEO of the company. One such way Tim reaches out to people is by offering to pray for them. There are numerous stories of Tim meeting with a client or employee who is noticeably downcast or experiencing some sort of turmoil in their life, whether it be from illness or family related issues. On other occasions, Tim has brought the whole office together to pray for an individual in their own office who is going through a particularly difficult time. In doing so, Tim ensures that the privacy of the individual is maintained. Actively praying for others has proven not only to foster cohesiveness among associates working at Tim Haahs, but it also helps to build a deeper and lasting commitment to the values that Tim Haahs has established in his firm. [prudence, justice]

Use your own money. Tim believes that one should use his or her own earned money to start a venture. Though he believes establishing and using a bank line of credit to absorb the ebbs and flows of cash is not bad, he does not believe partnering financially with equity or long-term debt provides the freedom and alignment one needs to pursue the firm's mission unencumbered. [prudence, temperance]

Proverbs 31:10-31 – While Tim was in the hospital waiting for his first heart transplant, part of his daily reading regimen included verses from the Bible. One chapter that stood out to him was Proverbs 31. In Proverbs 31, Tim saw a model for running a virtuous and fruitful business. In the person of the woman referenced throughout Proverbs 31, Tim saw his firm and its management. Likewise, in the actions of the husband referenced in Proverbs 31, he saw representations of how employees should treat his clients and view his business operations. The values espoused in this Proverb have helped Tim Haahs & Associates define and align itself with its mission. (All scriptures below are from *The Holy Bible* (NABRE), Proverbs 31 – verses are noted in superscript.)

[10]*Who can find a woman of worth?* *Far beyond jewels is her value.*
How do you find a company of worth? This is a question that is measured by things much deeper than solely the monetary wealth it creates. The answer to this question lies in a company's ability to build and maintain the highest quality employees, management, customers and competition. Integrity, competence, and ultimate service are all part of what makes a company of worth.
[11]*Her husband trusts her judgment;* *he does not lack income.* [12]*She brings him profit, not loss,* *all the days of her life.*
A company of worth is one whose clients will rely on its consultations. The customer's willingness to pay is evidence of the valued relationship between the company and its clients. Of course, those creating great value for clients are blessed with revenue in excess of the costs incurred to deliver the product or service. This creates a mutually beneficial, everlasting relationship.
[13]*She seeks out wool and flax* *and weaves with skillful hands.*
The company is always planning ahead to find the best resources in order to deliver the best results. This verse associates quality with the cost of the product or service to be delivered.

> [14]*Like a merchant fleet,*
> *she secures her provisions from afar.*

The company of worth will not cut corners in order to go great lengths for its clients. This is an additional emphasis on integrity in the business world. Many companies get caught up in the sale and the profits from a sale that they dismiss the long-term effects. A great company will price their products with the assurance that it is the best and this will secure a client who trusts the company's judgment.

> [15]*She rises while it is still night,*
> *and distributes food to her household,*
> *a portion to her maidservants.*

Leadership within a company of value will display a level of servant leadership in the workplace. Some examples of this are leaders who arrive at the office before the rest of the employees and leave after the last one leaves. This displays a level of commitment which creates a positive bond between the manager and his or her personnel.

> [16]*She picks out a field and acquires it;*
> *from her earnings she plants a vineyard.*

It is always important to be fiscally responsible to use the leaders' own earnings and hard work to build the foundation for a successful company. This is important because it ensures personal investment, proverbial skin in the game.

> [17]*She girds herself with strength;*
> *she exerts her arms with vigor.*

It is essential for the leaders to work hard, if not harder than everyone else in order to teach and serve the other employees.

> [18]*She enjoys the profit from her dealings;*
> *her lamp is never extinguished at night.*
> [19]*She puts her hands to the distaff,*
> *and her fingers ply the spindle.*

When there is work; employees are expected to work at 120%. When the times are rough employees will still be paid even if there are no projects. This is planned ahead of time to mitigate layoffs and develop trust between the company and her employees.

[20]*She reaches out her hands to the poor,* *and extends her arms to the needy.*
The company exists to help those in need. This premise encourages an internal climate of service and community and an external climate of social responsible and concern.
[21]*She is not concerned for her household when it snows—* *all her charges are doubly clothed.*
The company seeks to build up reserves from the past to ensure survival in times of 'famine.' This is a follow up from Proverb 31:18-19.
[22]*She makes her own coverlets;* *fine linen and purple are her clothing.*
It is an expectation that employees dress professionally with respect for themselves and others. There is an additional expectation to clean up after oneself at the office.
[23]*Her husband is prominent at the city gates* *as he sits with the elders of the land.*
The goal is to develop, serve and perform at such a level that it makes all clients look good to the point of recognition for the client in their respective professions.
[24]*She makes garments and sells them,* *and stocks the merchants with belts.* [25]*She is clothed with strength and dignity,* *and laughs at the days to come.*
The company is confident in who it is and where it is going.
[26]*She opens her mouth in wisdom;* *kindly instruction is on her tongue.*
Leadership is always loving but firm with staff, and staff members reciprocate that relationship with each other.
[27]*She watches over the affairs of her household,* *and does not eat the bread of idleness.*
The company promotes financial integrity and doesn't purchase or take what isn't owned or needed. Most of all it is never to be lazy in its dealings with its clients, management or employees.

28Her children rise up and call her blessed; her husband, too, praises her:
The leaders are praised for their interactions with her employees, stockholders, clients, suppliers, competitors, and society.
29"Many are the women of proven worth, but you have surpassed them all."
Humility in response to recognition is important.
30Charm is deceptive and beauty fleeting; the woman who fears the LORD is to be praised.
The truth is always revealed and one's success yesterday does not ensure one's success tomorrow. You cannot serve more than one master, so ensure you fulfill your mission with that one master.
31Acclaim her for the work of her hands, and let her deeds praise her at the city gates.
Because we are human and meant to receive, we appreciate the gifts this company of worth provides and she is praised for it.

The Bible verses laid out and explained above provided the content for Tim's first book, *P-31*, a best-seller in his native country of South Korea. Tim speaks internationally about the application of Proverbs 31 to business.

Business Practices

Recruiting and hiring. Hiring for "mission fit" is a critical success factor for Tim Haahs and Associates. Because of the rigorous hours and unique mission to serve those in need, candidates must fit a specific set of criteria. Interview questions about mission fit are behavioral based. Questions might take the form of an instruction like, "Tell me about a situation when you helped another in need."

Every candidate who reaches the final interview stage at the company is asked to read and reflect on Proverbs 31. During the final interview with Tim, the candidate is asked what he or she sees in this chapter and he shares his insights from years of study of this Proverb.

Business development through relationships. Tim and many at his firm intentionally build relationships outside of work through social events, not often a strength of technical professionals. The coaching, training, and on-going expectations around this activity have generated countless business opportunities for the firm. Tim's story and God's hand are at the center of this effort.

One story that Tim tells takes place at a wedding he officiated as the pastor. During the wedding reception, Tim took notice of a man sitting quietly across the table from him. Intentionally and out of habit, Tim made an effort to reach out to everyone at his table. When he reached this gentleman, he introduced himself, though the man knew he was the officiating pastor. Tim went beyond that and told the man (as he does with many people he meets) that he was a tentmaker. Curious, the man asked him further what he meant by being a tentmaker. Tim told the story of the Apostle Paul from the Bible and how Paul made tents to fund his ministry. Likewise, he started an engineering and architecture firm to support his own ministry. He then went deeper into his story about his heart transplants and why he started his own firm.

As fate would have it, the man at Tim's table was Vice President of Real Estate Design and Construction at the University of Pennsylvania Health System. The gentleman was so moved by Tim's story and willingness to sit down and talk with him, two weeks later, he called Tim and, without competitive bidding, asked Timothy Haahs & Associates to take on the new projects. [justice]

Hosting others, participation in their community as board members, and being good neighbors to all is at the root of their firm's success.

Planning for rigorous work. When Tim Haahs forecasts his fiscal years' goals and the related budgets, two significant assumptions are made: First, the financial year starts at zero. Though projects carryover from year-to-year, what was done last year is past and the new year is ripe with opportunity and the pressure to excel once again. Second, the staff workload is projected at 120% efficiency. This challenging work ethic is covered first in candidate interviews and the topic is approached in a very creative way. The candidates are asked if they would rather work for a firm that when work dries up, people are laid off, or a firm that would only consider laying people off as a last resort. Tim reports that almost all candidates prefer the latter. This transparent and forthright understanding and commitment allows the firm to save money for times when the workload is light.

Since most of the professional staff is salaried, they are expected to work long days to ensure quality, on-time service to the client, while the increased margin for the firm generates the wealth that funds reserves for times of 'famine' and the profit by which those in need are served. In this way, the bread of idleness is avoided.

During the real estate market collapse in 2008, engineering and architecture firms were known to lay-off as much as 50% of their professionals. Tim Haahs kept most of its team and kept its Miami, Florida office open, though its revenues suffered consistent with the market. The firm's metal was tested as pressure to reduce payroll was significant. The financial reserve that had been built-up through the firm's work-ethic to increase profit for the purpose of preparing for times of 'famine,' allowed the firm to carry involuntarily idle workers through the valley. Their retention through this period allowed the firm to leverage their capabilities coming out of the recession. The real execution of what had been theory (preparing for time of 'famine') served to improve trust among employees and an appreciation of why idleness must be avoided and excellence must be pursued. [prudence, temperance]

Collaboration with competitors. While aggressively pursuing market share for parking and multi-use related engineering and architecture projects in the Philadelphia region through his relationship-building, Tim Haahs humbly accepts work and welcomes collaboration with other firms; sometimes even when it doesn't make sense. Tim shared a story that was captured in a movie short that illustrates an extraordinary concern for others . . . even competitors. A larger firm was competing with Tim Haahs & Associates for a job that

Tim's firm won. After the announcement, the competing firm owner came to Tim and shared that his firm was close to bankruptcy. Tim listened and had to face the nagging pressure of his mission, against the temptation to do damage to the enemy, a competing firm!

After discussion and with the reluctant trust of his Board, Tim shared a significant part of the contract with the competing firm so that they might live another day and survive for the benefit of the employees and families thereof. Tim recalls Proverbs 25:21-22 (*The Holy Bible* – NIV) addressing how to treat your enemy. "It is like pouring hot coals over their eyes, and the Lord will reward you."[180] No mission gimmick here. [courage, temperance, justice]

Company rituals. Company rituals are important in any enterprise. Rituals are the events that help define the culture and reinforce the common values and relationships among employees. Tim Haahs hosts two significant annual rituals. One is a summer retreat where firm leaders and employees gather to celebrate one another, their accomplishments, and explore pursuit of the firm's mission. The second is the firm's Christmas party that is hosted at the company headquarters and includes the church facilities therein. Employees, spouses, significant others, customers, vendors, and friends are invited to share food, drink, and enjoy world-class entertainment with the Timothy Haahs & Associates family. All invitations are signed personally for an added touch of closeness and meaning.

Employee Benefits. Sometimes, the benefits of employees are nominalized by employers and taken for granted by employees. This is especially true when the government chooses to offer competing benefits. Tim Haahs enhances benefits to employees through its church-run day care on premises, offered to employees for a lower-than-market cost. Usually, only large firms can afford such an undertaking and minimize the impact of any financial risk in hosting a day care. [courage, justice]

Employees choosing to commit to a not-for-profit effort serving those in need are offered cash and in-kind matching gifts, as well as stipends for significant involvement in major non-profit projects. [justice, temperance] Based upon firm results, employees are offered lucrative bonuses intended to reward them for their hard work and dedication. [justice, temperance]

Price-for-value. The intentional relationship-building and story-sharing with potential clients enhances the brand image of the firm immensely. What might have been a cold call for one firm trying to solicit business, becomes a 'warm call' for Tim Haahs due to the widespread knowledge of the firm and his story. This brand equity, in turn, allows the firm to price its services at a premium, though not out of competitive bounds, and fuels its pursuit of its mission and desire for reserves when bad times come. Staying true and integral to the mission is critical, as any deviation could be viewed with doubt and cynicism. Constancy of purpose is critical. [prudence]

Superior service. With the full alignment of mission, expectations, compensation, stipends, bonuses, and benefits, the engineering and architecture professionals at Tim Haahs can focus on delivering on their promise of 'distinguished' work. With employees ready and margin sufficient to absorb unforeseen project needs, Tim Haahs professionals can respond to emergencies without hesitation.

Tim shared this story during our visit. His firm had designed a parking structure for a university campus in Tennessee. The construction company, to which Tim Haahs is not affiliated, missed putting reinforcing steel ties in some of the vertical columns. Because the architectural drawings were complete, all the liability rested squarely on the construction company. Going the extra mile, Tim Haahs professionals jumped into action and proposed a cost-effective, efficient, and acceptable remedy, using carbon fiber wraps, that served both the construction company and the client well. Though they invested weeks of time in additional project management and consulting, they did so only to help rescue the situation with no additional billings or change orders – simply because they believe in going the extra mile. This kind of effort has served them well and manifested in numerous client referrals, growing their business. [temperance, prudence, justice, courage]

Give back. Giving to local and regional non-profits is expected as the outward manifestation of its mission. Charitable efforts like

Toys for Tots, HeartWalk, American Heart Association, Jaisohn Foundation, Elijah Promise, Big Brothers/Big Sisters of America, Habitat for Humanity, and many other Christian organizations have been perennial beneficiaries of the work of Tim Haahs & Associates.

Defining moments. There is a 'consciousness of concern' for those in their offices and those in relationship with employees, whether friends or family. It seems that everyone is looking for those defining moments when the firm can behave in an irrational way to evidence its mission. Employees spoke of times when the firm intervened during client illness, employee child illnesses, or when a friend of employees had suffered great tragedy. While we were at the firm, an employee had a friend who had been killed in a vehicle accident and during the company-sponsored lunch, the entire company prayed for the victim's family, and the employee who was suffering. Acting on defining moments gives their mission life.

Initially, the firm did not do work for casinos. Tim tells the story of the day when one of his employees brought a challenge to him. He knew this employee was working to market to a developer for design work on a large project. He did not know the project was a casino project. The employee confessed to Tim that the project was for a casino and that she was getting advice from her Christian small group to leave the company because of the nature of this particular customer. Not wanting to leave, she felt torn.

Initially, he was going stop the marketing effort, but then he received wisdom. He asked the employee to return to her group and ask if any of the products and/or services her group members provide are consumed in-or-for casinos. After some consideration, the group altered their judgment of the firm and the employee, and generously apologized. Sometimes critical alignment is evidenced by what you choose not to do, supported by wisdom. [prudence]

Over communicate and give the work away. Trust-building is a continual process at Tim Haahs. Many businesspeople view trust as something to give away carte blanche, and others hoard it for fear that others will abuse it. Tim Haahs gives it away when it is deserved, and when you are trusted, the opportunities to grow are amazing!

Rachel Yoka, Tim's Vice President of Strategic Business Planning attributes all her opportunities while at Tim Haahs and Associates to Tim's trust in her abilities and openness to new ideas. She shared with us a time when Tim had a conflicting church appointment with a United Nations presentation he was to give. Because Tim holds his faith and commitment to the church a priority, he decided to attend the church function and asked Rachel to present at the United Nations function instead and deliver his presentation. Not only was that an indication of Tim's priorities, but it was also a huge display of confidence and trust in Rachel's abilities and allowed her to refine her own speaking and presentation skills. [prudence, justice]

Though accountability for decisions is very centralized, once Tim has made up his mind how the company is going to operate or handle a particular situation, he takes the time to explain his rationale supporting the decision so others have an opportunity to understand his argument and hopefully come to the same conclusion in the future. Each of Tim's decisions can be tied back to the firm's core values and beliefs. There is not a lot of room for dissenters, as explanations are thorough and consistent and reinforce the culture of the firm. [prudence, courage]

Closing Thoughts

The culture at Tim Haahs & Associates is incredibly unique. The fact that a church and his business share space, with his office doors opening to both is perhaps one-of-a-kind. His two heart transplants and his growing up in a leper colony (yes, but that's another story) are enough to warrant another look. But it's the firm's values and business practices that any enterprise can adopt that have made the firm the success it is.

Clients of service businesses like Tim Haahs & Associates benefit just from the distinguished service offered them. Sometimes they benefit even more. Here is a final story how serving others well does good. The firm had just finished up a project at a national pharmaceutical company and his client asked the team to dinner. At the dinner, Tim stood up to toast his client as he didn't know exactly why they were at dinner except for the fact that they had just completed the project together. Tim was ready to speak when his client interrupted Tim and politely asked him to sit down. He proceeded to toast Tim and his company for their work. The client shared with the group that he had been called into his boss's office that week and was applauded for doing an excellent job with the project and maintaining a level head throughout the difficult undertaking. Going the extra mile, returning phone calls the same day, and keeping everyone informed reflected well on the client. So well, in fact, that with the Tim Haahs team present, the client announced that he had been promoted to the Director of Facilities based upon the outcome of the project.

Serving those in need cannot be just words. When a business leader really means it and lives it, the results can be astounding and expansive. Virtues and values in the workplace give meaning to work that inspires commitment of all to the work at hand, bringing enumerable rewards to the firm. Proverbs 31 lives!

Charting a Course for the Whole Person
Compass Financial Resources
Olathe, Kansas

Company History

Russ Lane, the founder and CEO of Compass Financial Resources, LLC began his career about as far away from financial services as one could get, as a history teacher and athletic coach. Yet, some of Russ's future beliefs and values about performance and compensation were forged when he was working in this teaching/coaching vocation. Even though he enjoyed teaching very much, he was discontent with the fact that 1) he could not make a living enough to support his family doing something very important, and 2) that a hard-working, fully committed teacher like him was not compensated commensurate with the work he put in, especially compared to his more tenured peers who did significantly less and were paid significantly more.

As many teachers do, he chose to supplement his meager school-year earnings with summer employment. Some of his peers had developed a relationship with Franklin Financial Services as financial advisors and he chose to follow suit. The necessity for enhanced income gave Russ the experience and the courage he would need to make financial services his career and would ultimately lead him to create his own company.

Russ' financial advising career got off to an auspicious start, batting .000; 0 for 34. He wondered if he could ever make a career of this! The firm offered little to no training for representatives like him and reps had to perform every aspect of the sale from lead generation to closing and follow-up, making for an exceptionally long learning curve. Undeterred, though with doubt creeping in, he promised himself that when he got stood-up for an appointment (which happened often in those early days), he would go door-to-door and meet people and ask if he could be of service. He remembers fondly that some of his best clients over the years have been people he met going door-to-door in the early years.

As the years rolled-on, Russ began to develop a sizable base of clientele doing financial services only in the summer. With his current base, solid experience, and what seemed like limitless opportunities to do more, he chose to abandon the teaching/coaching profession and become a financial services advisor full-time with Franklin. As his clientele became more diverse, he found himself unable to meet the needs of others with the narrow product offering provided by Franklin as a sole source. He had a choice to make: stay safe with Franklin and push products on others that didn't match their needs perfectly, or set out on his own where he could shop for and provide a variety of products from a variety of sources that served his clients better. His desire to serve his clients better easily won out, despite the absence of whatever safety net Franklin Financial Services offered.

Russ named his firm Compass Financial Resources with some aforethought, and on the heels of hearing a Navy Seal talk about the first step one must accomplish when lost and needing to find your way back or home: figure out where you are. He believed the compass imagery fit the emphasis Russ wanted in the firm; a holistic view of clients as people, not just as customers, helping them chart a course for financial freedom and peace of mind. He explains that when starting out, a one or two degree of deviation can lead one later in their financial journey to a vastly different place than where they want to be.

Success has accompanied the firm's effort, and he gives much credit to his talented and committed team of advisors and associates for their hard work and sacrificial contributions to the firm's mission. As of 2020, the firm now employees 18 advisors and has over $600 million in assets under management (AUM). They have expanded to branch offices in Hutchinson, Kansas; Lincoln, Nebraska; and Hannibal, Missouri.

Underlying Values and Beliefs

Like any business leader, providing a clear mission and vision, supported with values by which the firm will do business provides the foundation of what Compass Financial Resources is today. His experience and passion for educators fuels the target of the firm's effort. Though the mission and vision are refreshed periodically, here is how Russ describes why Compass Financial Resources exists:

Mission: To provide financial peace of mind while giving greater glory to God.

Vision: To be the best in the world at providing financial information and resources to educators.

Here are some of the values Russ and his team define for Compass. The cardinal virtues most closely associated with the values are provided in brackets.

Life balance. In his own life, and, thus for those working within Compass, Russ desires people to value faith, family, fitness, and finance – in balance. It was evident that Russ lives these values personally and models them for his employees. As a father and husband, Russ takes his role seriously and seeks to love and provide for his family as best as he can.

As an extension of his family after raising four children of their own, Russ and his wife, Annette, adopted a special-needs daughter from Guatemala, Kimber Rose. He has made specific decisions, not the least of which was to start Compass, to better serve his family. Russ tries to keep himself in great physical condition, though he'll admit often he's the "best-in-shape fat guy he knows." His exercise time is used to center his day. Finally, he makes an effort to be financially stable to support his family, the church, and the not-for-profit charity he founded. [temperance, justice, prudence]

Life-long learning. Russ spends time studying the best of his industry and has participated in a variety of mentoring relationships that require investment and demand accountability. Russ likens this to sharpening his saw. He has been able to build others up as he develops his own knowledge. [prudence]

'A'-level performers. Russ expects a high level of performance from his team and associates. He comments that while some people may naturally give up on themselves, they are less likely to give up on a team member. This belief has manifested itself deeply in the unique teamwork Russ has implemented at Compass (see Business Practices). [prudence]

Leadership. His leadership method continues to evolve, but it is often enhanced as he studies the leadership success of others. Russ mentioned Mel Gibson in his role in the movie, *We Were Soldiers*. During the movie, Mel Gibson (as Colonel Moore) shares with his men that he will be the first one on the battlefield and the last one off. It's important to Russ that his associates know he is there for them and that he will tirelessly support them in pursuit of the firm's mission.

Russ also mentioned Lou Holtz, former Head Football Coach at the University of Notre Dame. After winning a national championship, Coach Holtz reported that his primary regret was that he sought to maintain the status quo vs. continue to lead the team's pursuit of excellence. Russ has committed to not making the same mistake. [prudence]

Humility. Consistent with Russ' practice of his faith, Russ invests time in daily Mass and asks specifically for humility. With his personal success and the success of Compass as a whole, he fears the onset of arrogance and hubris. It's the downfall of many a company. He adds that amidst all the craziness of a workday, it's nice to calm down and focus on that which is most important.

Russ is a faithful Catholic and has a particularly strong devotion to Saint (Mother) Teresa. He shared a story about Mother Teresa when she was returning to India after having been awarded the Nobel Peace Prize. Her fellow Sisters could not find her on the plane for some time. Fearing something had happened, her Sisters alerted the flight attendants and a search began. They found her on her hands and knees cleaning the bathrooms at the back of the plane. When asked if she were okay, she responded that sometimes to maintain humility, one needs to be humiliated. In a deep sense, she knew the damage that could come with the earthly manifestations of success. This example has helped inform Russ' pursuit of humility. [prudence]

Build trust. Trust with his people is paramount. Russ takes every opportunity to build and instill trust. The manifestation of trust has likely been the single greatest contributor to the unique teamwork model practiced at the firm. His trust-building mantra is, "Be more than fair." When sharing commissions with his team, he will often ask, "How much do you think your work was worth?" He'll listen and has historically bumped-up the request where deserved. His belief is that as long as his employees see that he is fair, ethical, and honest with them, then he can successfully combat pride, greed and envy that too often accompany success. [prudence, temperance, justice]

Business Practices

Unique teamwork. Compass has implemented and built on some industry-best practices related to teamwork. This is no small feat and requires an extraordinary amount of trust. In the financial services industry, 'producers' or licensed financial advisors are rewarded for selling financial products to clients with sale and on-going future commissions earned. This has bred two behaviors that make teamwork difficult in this industry: you 'eat what you kill' mindset, with little thought for others, and producer arrogance that it is their work alone that generates income.

Russ wanted something different in order to serve Compass' clients better. Traditionally, a producer executes the entire process from lead generation to closing, though not all producers are 'A' players at each of the functions. Remember Russ' experience working for Franklin where he was expected to be both head chef and bottle washer? For instance, Russ is good at teaching the client and initiating relationships. He is not as good at securing a client's financial history, nor at analyzing the history in a way that the best financial products can easily be selected for the client. He envisioned a 'shared commission' structure that would allow multiple participants to enjoy a portion of a full commission for their relative contribution to a client's case. Alignment of compensation to strategies to execute a company's mission is an important factor for success of any enterprise, but this would require licensed professional advisors to receive less of a commission on cases that they had generated. Instead of cashing their usually large individual commission checks, they'd throw their commission checks into a pool to be redistributed to all those participating in the collection of successful cases.

In dogged pursuit of what was best, not only in financial products, but in service to clients leveraging the different strengths of those on the Compass team, Russ earned the trust of his team members and convinced them that this approach would be best for Compass' clients and for all the people on the team. Some were doubtful at the time, though they trusted enough to give it a try. As evidence of his commitment to the idea, Russ would frequently give others a higher percentage of a case commission than perhaps was initially agreed. Without trust there is no way this unique teamwork would manifest.

Today, all producers and team members are said to earn significantly more than they would make otherwise using this approach. Their humility and trust of one another has generated extraordinary competitive advantage. In 2019, earnings for the advisors were four-to-five times more than had they worked by themselves on all facts of their cases. [prudence, justice, temperance, courage]

Developing people. Though the expectation of the firm is that everyone performs at an 'A' level, not everyone starts out there. With Russ' history of seeking mentoring, he provides the same service for those who aspire to be 'A' level players. He sets aside time to coach others and frequently brings gems of wisdom from his resources for consideration by all in attendance. He shared a story where he was reviewing a final client report and was not pleased with the result. Appropriately he asked, "Is this the best report you can create?" Receiving both the criticism and challenge with humility, the team member went back to work and produced something significantly better. An environment where learning and teachability are present creates the stage for quick and real improvement. [justice, prudence]

There have been times where Russ' desire for another's success has outstripped his reason to halt investment in that person, even to the point of enabling the person. While he regrets these times, he admits that erring on that side of the equation is better than cutting one's development too soon and failing them by not allowing the full manifestation of their God-given talents and flourishing. [prudence]

Modeling client expectations. Russ expects all Compass' team members to live a balanced life of faith, family, fitness, and finance. Specifically related to finance, he expects all team members to be their proverbial "best client" and practice what they preach. This expectation enhances advisor integrity and breeds confidence as the team approaches clients about their financial futures. [temperance, prudence]

Dignity of others. As a Catholic man who happens to run a financial services business, and a highly successful one at that, Russ has chosen to do more than what he could have ever envisioned he could do by helping others around the world. His interest in and devotion to Saint (Mother) Teresa led him to a relationship with Father Vijay from a small town in southeastern India. Father Vijay had the opportunity to spend time with Mother Teresa during her life and ministry. Toward the end of her life, she pulled Father Vijay aside and asked him to promise to care for the poor and orphans in India.

This was attractive to Russ. Though his afternoon after a Mass was spoken for with a planned trip to the lake for relaxation with his family, Russ felt called to invite Father Vijay to join them. As Russ shares, Father Vijay was not as excited to join him as Russ might have been, but he did so anyway!

Little did either of them know, that that spontaneous encounter would lead to the establishment of a combined senior center and orphanage called Valley of Smiles, in the small town where Father Vijay ministers. Over the last five years, Russ, Compass associates, and numerous clients have given irrationally to build this community center. Russ and others have traveled there several times to reap the blessings of giving. He has used his resources and influence to bring dignity to the poor and the often neglected halfway around the world.

Russ shares that 100% of the contributions from others go to the direct benefit of Valley of Smiles. He funds any overhead costs out of his own reserves. He recalls the instruction from Saint (Mother) Teresa, "Give until it hurts." [justice, temperance]

Concluding Thoughts

Russ' personal virtue and conviction have led to a highly successful financial services business. The courage and wisdom to align compensation with the goals of the firm in service to clients is nothing short of remarkable where individual reward and compensation is at the heart of the industry. The trust foundation required to execute this change demanded a concern for others and humility beyond normal reason.

When virtues are practiced at work, clients win and employees and associates win. So, too, can others less fortunate half-a-world away. Business, as intended, is a force for good and a force for God.

CHAPTER 8

The Transcendent Business

❦

"He is no fool who gives that which he cannot keep, to gain what he cannot lose." – missionary martyr, Jim Elliott

IN THE U.S. TODAY, the current trajectory of economics, politics, and religion is untenable. The stubborn pursuit of limited government by the Libertarians and the naïve pursuit of government-led solutions to social justice by the Democratic Socialists polarize our nation. These extreme stances, perhaps one taken to counterbalance the other, slowly gnaw away at our individual freedom and liberty. In one case, freedom and liberty will be taken from us by those marginalized in society, and in the other, they will be taken by an all-controlling government.

Socialism is a lagging indicator of injustice. The debate is no longer about the pursuit of social justice. The argument is about the means to that end and socialism is not the answer. But because business is dismissed by the greater culture as a means to that end primarily due to its post-Enlightenment abuses and perversions, it no longer registers on the radar of options. Yet truth would hold out business-reclaiming-its-divine-purpose as the means of choice. Without it, what other viable option exists?

Adam Smith saw us clearly. Heed his warnings. Reject his folly as prophetic as it was. No fixed set of moral rules, no well-functioning free markets.

The health and vibrancy of a society is a function of the health and vibrancy of its institutions, and because business arguably is its largest institution, the health of our United States depends significantly on the moral health of business. The moral health of business is manifested in and through business leaders. It is time for us to get healthy as business leaders!

Yes, organizational health trumps everything, but organizations don't behave; people do. We, as individual Christian businessmen and women hold the reins and will write (and right) the end of this story. Without our "righting," the end is predictable and consistent with socialism's history. If we fail, the acknowledged leadership of the free world and the shining global light for freedom and liberty will be dimmed, if not extinguished.

Millennials, among others, insist on meaningful work and purpose beyond profit. Leading with a focus on optimizing cooperation will help your business create more value, and consequently, more wealth, demanding more virtue. You've read stories of what business leaders who practice virtue have done with their businesses. Yes, stop our slow burn toward socialism, reverse course, and in the process, build a prevailing and purposeful business that impacts all stakeholders and leaves a lasting legacy.

Observable hypocrisy by those professing the Christian/Catholic faith has diminished the influence and impact of Christ's church. Too often this hypocrisy is on display in the daily practice of our businesses operated on the false ideology that its purpose is to maximize shareholder wealth. Moral relativism absent truth made way for this ideology and will persist until courageous Christian business leaders expose it to light. As a Christian/Catholic business leader, it is to this transcendent purpose we are called.

Here are the tenets required to build and sustain a transcendent business:

13 Tenets of a Transcendent Business

A Transcendent Business and its leaders . . .

I.   Practice virtue at work. They practice prudence, temperance, justice, and fortitude perfected by faith, hope, and love. Prudence, knowing the right thing to do and acting on it, provides the fixed set of moral rules required for a well-functioning free market.

II. Acknowledge the presence of social injustice and reject the notion that central control of means or distribution germane to socialism is not a viable solution. The injection of Christian love into the economic sector is the answer.

III. View the purpose of business beyond the narrow and shallow purpose defined by the dominant ideology – to maximize shareholder wealth. They align their priorities, their values, and their enterprise culture to this redefined purpose.

IV. Embrace their responsibility for the physical, emotional, and spiritual health of those entrusted to their employ.

V.   Practice justice that demands each person receive his or her due as one created in the image of God and adjusts their policies and practices to align with this concept. They also understand that there are real limits that could put their business enterprise at risk and practice justice within those boundaries.

VI. Temper the onset of pride and do whatever is possible to reduce the response of envy in others to not draw others into sin.

VII. View people as ends in-and-of-themselves; not simply as means to be used in the pursuit of profit. The flourishing of human beings is the ultimate purpose of a transcendent business. This requires leaders to be clear, authentic, vulnerable, and empathetic.

VIII. Accept their responsibility to protect human dignity in the economic sector and pursue the common good in lieu of abdicating that responsibility to the State or government. This is the manifestation of the Catholic Social Teaching principle of subsidiarity and the Biblical principle of loving your neighbor.

IX. Lead with the specific intent of optimizing cooperation. They recognize that self-discipline is a pre-requisite to effective leadership and that as soon as others are needed to do the work, the primary constraint in their business changes to optimizing cooperation. This connects overtly to concern for the flourishing of employees and other stakeholders in the business.

X. Pursue solidarity with the poor and underserved in their communities by offering jobs or training programs and create opportunities for employment while protecting the dignity of those in the condition of poverty.

XI. Recognize the need for "patient capital" and the good of diminishing negative returns over a longer period of time to solve some of the world's and our communities' biggest problems.

XII. Earn the trust of workers and create an environment of mutual benefit, justice, and concern for one another centered on mutual respect and service to their collective clients or customers. This applies especially in environments where workers have organized against management – perpetuating the "great mistake."

XIII. Seek to add their own thumbprint as Virtuosos and compete well in ways that bring flourishing to all stakeholders and glory to God in the process.

How do I respond?

Here are a few thoughts to questions that may be weighing heavily on your mind.

As a Christian/Catholic business leader I am feeling convicted (not condemned). What can I do to address this?

As Christians, we always have at our disposal the divine mercy of Jesus Christ. Repent and reconcile. Do so with a contrite heart and change going forward. Ask for wisdom and prudence on your journey. Share this change with those close to you for accountability. For more growth and acceleration, join a CEO or executive accountability group like Acumen (www.acumenimpact.com). Too much is at stake for you to not forgive yourself as Christ will forgive you and move forward with strength and courage.

I get this, but my shareholders don't or won't. How do I address this preeminent stakeholder?

If you are an owner or on the Board of Directors, become a "Virtue Activist." Expect your management team to be virtuous (wise, just, temperate, and courageous). Expect nothing less. Help them translate virtues into beliefs, values, paradigms, and behaviors. It is likely those knowing of and practicing the virtues of faith, hope, and love may help accelerate progress. Temper the pursuit of short-term results at the expense of long-term benefits for all stakeholders. Ensure executive leaders lead through the filter of optimizing cooperation. Your mission? Prioritize people. Buy them a book about this and offer to discuss the contents.

I am an employee who has been subject to mistakes of business leaders absent truth. How do I overcome being jaded and how do I improve my relationships with my bosses while speaking the truth?

Pray for your boss or bosses. Pray that the truth would shine on their beliefs, values, paradigms, and practices. Converse with them about how essential it is to prioritize people and to have a fixed set of moral rules to protect individual liberty and free markets. Buy them a book about this and discuss the contents. Prepare well for the time you take greater reins in your business. Your time is coming.

I'm not in business but have influence in my church. What can I do to engage other business leaders with this truth?

My experience says many business leaders are underutilized in their churches; especially leveraging their core competencies in business. Convene a group of businessmen and women and talk about patient capital and how much more could be done to protect human dignity, pursue the common good, and solve some of our communities' biggest problems if we were to create businesses and jobs for those in our communities. You can leverage Significant Matters (www. significantmatters.com) to lead this discussion and the mobilization of businesspeople toward this mission.

Now Educated

So, what will you do? You can do nothing and stay the course, or you can embark on this wonderful journey toward virtue and holiness at work. The one thing you can no longer do is plead ignorance. You know too much! There is an option to what-is in business and so much is at stake if we accept the status quo as enough. The value of livelihoods and fortunes to be gained in business pale in comparison to the blessings and souls to be touched as you pursue this work.

Truth is the light unto your path. God has not been silent. We simply have chosen to listen to others. If your journey toward a transcendent business is just beginning, I hope this book gives you fuel and vision for the journey – oil for your lamps, if you will. If already started, then I hope this book provides more of a foundation to support your efforts philosophically, economically, and most important, Biblically and instructionally from the Church. If you are called to business as a Christian, pursue your vocation with a fervor and commitment deserving of our Creator and our Savior, Jesus Christ. The future of freedom, liberty, and the pursuit of happiness for all depends on it. To God be the glory!

You are no fool.

ABOUT THE AUTHOR

Dave Geenens is Associate Professor in the School of Business at Benedictine College in Atchison, Kansas. Simultaneous to much of his academic career spanning 11-plus years, Dave has consulted with and held part-time executive positions in business enterprises in a variety of industries including apparel manufacturing and decoration, financial advising, equipment manufacturing, and large-scale commercial services.

His full-time business executive experience includes President/CFO of Fire Door Solutions and CEO of Avascend Healthcare Hospitality, both in Overland Park, KS; CEO/President of Impact

Design in Lansing, KS; Vice President of Operations at Penn Emblem (Philadelphia, PA) and Gear for Sports (Lenexa, KS.) Each of these business leadership experiences coupled with his Christian faith have informed his hands-on application of the principles in this book.

Dave holds a bachelor's degree and MBA along with a CPA license (inactive).

He is the author of three other books:

- *Nothing is Free – The Price Only Business Leaders Can Pay to Protect Free Markets*
- *Leaderslip – Reversing the Slide of American Enterprise Leadership*
- *Arise! – Life Changing Truths for the Tormented Leader*

Dave speaks to companies and groups nationally about the integration of faith and work and the critical role Christian virtue plays in the protection of free markets and liberty, and how virtue is essential for effective leadership and optimizing cooperation.

He and his wife, Terry, and their dog, Lucy, live in Lenexa, Kansas (Kansas City) as empty nesters. They love and enjoy their grown children; Megan, Aubrey, and Austin; their spouses, grandchildren, and grand dogs.

ENDNOTES

1 Saint John Paul II, Encyclical Letter, *Centesimus Annus*, 43.

2 Michael Novak, *Business as a Calling*, p. 5.

3 Pope Francis, Encyclical Letter, *Evangelii Gaudium*, 203.

4 Timothy Cardinal Dolan, *The Pope's Case for Virtuous Capitalism*, news article.

5 Adam Smith, *An Inquiry into the Nature and Causes of the Wealth of Nations*, Book 1, Chapter 2: Of the Principle which gives Occasion to the Division of Labour.

6 Russell Roberts, *How Adam Smith Can Change Your Life*, Penguin Group, 2014, p. 20.

7 Smith, *An Inquiry into the Nature and Causes of the Wealth of Nations*, Book 1, Chapter 2: Of the Principle which gives Occasion to the Division of Labour.

8 Roberts, p. 229.

9 Roberts, p. 225.

10 *"Hume on Religion"*. *Stanford Encyclopedia of Philosophy*. Retrieved 26 May 2008.

11 https://www.oxfordhandbooks.com/view/10.1093/oxfordhb/9780199605064.001.0001/oxfordhb-9780199605064-e-23

12 James R. Otteson, *What Adam Smith Knew – Moral Lessons on Capitalism from its Greatest Champions and Fiercest Opponents*, Encounter Books, 2014, p. 130. (excerpted from David Hume, *A Treatise of Human Nature*, Book III, Part II: Of Justice and Injustice, sections 1-2, 1739-40)

13 Otteson, p. 130.

14 Otteson, p. 130.

15 Otteson, p. 130.

16 Otteson, p. 139.

17   Roberts, p. 229.

18   Otteson, p. 131.

19   Otteson, p. 143.

20   Otteson, p. 139.

21   Pope Leo XIII, Encylical Letter *Rerum Novarum*, 1891, 3.

22   Pope Leo XIII, 4.

23   Fr. Matthew Habiger, OSB, *Papal Teaching on Private Property*, University Press of America, Inc., 1990, p. 9.

24   Pope Leo XIII, 8.

25   Pope Leo XIII, 11.

26   Adam Smith, *The Theory of Moral Sentiments*, Chapter III, Of the Influences and Authority of Conscience.

27   Roberts, p 94.

28   Roberts, p. 229.

29   Roberts, p. 1.

30   Otteson, p. 25. (excerpted from Adam Smith, *The Theory of Moral Sentiments*, Chapter 2, Of the sense of Justice, of Remorse, and the consciousness of Merit, paragraphs 1 -2, 1759)

31   Roberts, p. 26.

32   Smith, *The Theory of Moral Sentiments*, Chapter II, Of the Love of Praise, and of that of Praise-worthiness; and the Dread of Blame, and of that of Blame-worthiness.

33   Roberts, p. 40.

34   Robert L. Heilbroner, *The Essential Adam Smith*, Norton, 1986, p. 69. (excerpted from Adam Smith, *The Theory of Moral Sentiments*, Part 1, Of the Propriety of Action Consisting of Three Sections, Section I, Of the Sense of Propriety, Chapter 1, Of Sympathy, 1759)

35   Heilbroner, p. 72 (excerpted from Adam Smith, *The Theory of Moral Sentiments*, Part 1, Of the Propriety of Action Consisting of Three Sections, Section I, Of the Sense of Propriety, Chapter 3, Of the manner in which we judge of the propriety or impropriety of the affections of other men, by their concord or dissonance with our own, 1759)

36   Roberts, p. 124.

37   Roberts, p. 46.

38   Brene Brown, *Braving the Wilderness*, 2017 Random House, p. 31-33.

39   Roberts, p. 56.

40   Roberts, p. 58.

41   Roberts, p. 60.

42   Roberts, p. 96.

43   Roberts, p. 99.

44   Roberts, p. 102.

45   Roberts, p. 140.

46   Heilbroner, p. 77 (excerpted from Adam Smith, *The Theory of Moral Sentiments*, Part 1, Of the Propriety of Action Consisting of Three Sections, Section I, Of the Sense of Propriety, Chapter 5, Of the amiable and respectable virtues, 1759)

47   Heilbroner, p. 72 (excerpted from Adam Smith, *The Theory of Moral Sentiments*, Part 1, Of the Propriety of Action Consisting of Three Sections, Section I, Of the Sense of Propriety, Chapter 3, Of the manner in which we judge of the propriety or impropriety of the affections of other men, by their concord or dissonance with our own, 1759)

48   Roberts, p. 218.

49   Roberts, p. 219.

50   Roberts, p. 30.

51   Roberts, p. 124.

52   Chris Stefanick, *Absolute Relativism*, Catholic Answers, 2011, p. 1.

53   Stefanick, p. 2.

54   Pope Emeritus Benedict XVI, address to the participants in the Ecclesial Diocesan Convention of Rome, June 6, 2005.

55   Stefanick, p. 20.

56   Roberts, p. 55.

57   Brown, p. 32.

58   Roberts, p. 89.

59   https://www.apa.org/topics/divorce/

60   Saint John Paul II, Encyclical Letter *Centesimus Annus*, 35.

61   Cardinal Peter K.A. Turkson, *Vocation of the Business Leader – A Reflection*, Pontifical Council of Justice and Peace, 51.

62   Heilbroner, p. 58. (Authors commentary on excerpts from Adam Smith, *The Theory of Moral Sentiments*)

63   Heilbroner, p. 58. (Authors commentary on excerpts from Adam Smith, *The Theory of Moral Sentiments*)

64   Heilbroner, p. 65 (excerpted from Adam Smith, *The Theory of Moral Sentiments*, Part 1, Of the Propriety of Action Consisting of Three Sections, Section I, Of the Sense of Propriety, Chapter 1, Of Sympathy, 1759)

65   Heilbroner, p. 59 (Authors commentary on excerpts from Adam Smith, *The Theory of Moral Sentiments*)

66 Heilbroner, p. 75 (excerpted from Adam Smith, *The Theory of Moral Sentiments*, Part 1, Of the Propriety of Action Consisting of Three Sections, Section I, Of the Sense of Propriety, Chapter 4, Of the manner in which we judge of the propriety or impropriety of the affections of other men, by their concord or dissonance with our own, 1759)

67 Heilbroner, p. 86 (excerpted from Adam Smith, *The Theory of Moral Sentiments*, Part 1, Of the Propriety of Action Consisting of Three Sections, Section III, Of the Effects of Prosperity and Adversity upon the Judgment of Mankind with regard to the Propriety of Action; and why it is more easy to obtain their Approbation in the one state than in the other, Chapter 3, Of the corruption of our moral sentiments, which is occasioned by this disposition to admire the rich and the great, and to despise or neglect persons of poor and mean condition, 1759)

68 Heilbroner, p. 81 (excerpted from Adam Smith, *The Theory of Moral Sentiments*, Part 1, Of the Propriety of Action Consisting of Three Sections, Section III, Of the Effects of Prosperity and Adversity upon the Judgment of Mankind with regard to the Propriety of Action; and why it is more easy to obtain their Approbation in the one state than in the other, Chapter 2, Of the origin of Ambition, and of the distinction of Ranks, 1759)

69 Adam Smith, *An Inquiry into the Nature and Causes of the Wealth of Nations*, Book 1, Chapter 2: Of the Principle which gives Occasion to the Division of Labour.

70 Heilbroner, p. 85 (excerpted from Adam Smith, *The Theory of Moral Sentiments*, Part 1, Of the Propriety of Action Consisting of Three Sections, Section III, Of the Effects of Prosperity and Adversity upon the Judgment of Mankind with regard to the Propriety of Action; and why it is more easy to obtain their Approbation in the one state than in the other, Chapter 2, Of the origin of Ambition, and of the distinction of Ranks, 1759)

71 Heilbroner, p. 85.

72 Heilbroner, p. 69 (excerpted from Adam Smith, *The Theory of Moral Sentiments*, Part 1, Of the Propriety of Action Consisting of Three Sections, Section I, Of the Sense of Propriety, Chapter 1, Of Sympathy, 1759)

73 *The Holy Bible* (NIV), Matthew 10:39.

74 https://www.bibleinfo.com/en/questions/what-are-seven-deadly-sins

75 *The Holy Bible* (NIV), Matthew 5:19.

76 Roberts, p. 134.

77 Samuel Gregg, *Tea Party Catholic*, Crossroads Publishing, 2013, p. 102. (see Saint John Paul II, Encyclical Letter, *Sollicitudo Rei Socialis*, 38, 1987)

78 Michael Matheson Miller, SAT Talks, www.sattalks.org, The Videos, 2015.

79 Gregg, p. 103.

80 Gregg, p. 103.

81 Timothy Cardinal Dolan.

82 Gregg, p. 103.

83 Gregg, p. 102.

84 F.A. Hayek, *The Road to Serfdom*.

85 Pope Pius XI, Encyclical Letter, *Divini Redemptoris*, 8, 1937.

86 Pope Pius XI, 61.

87 Pope Pius XI, 9.

88 Pope Pius XI, 57.

89 F.A. Hayek, *The Road to Serfdom – The Definitive Edition*, University of Chicago Press, 1992, p. 66.

90 Hayek, p. 76.

91 Hayek, p. 71.

92 Hayek, p. 71.

93 Hayek, p. 72.

94 Hayek, p. 72

95 Hayek, p. 77.

96 Hayek, p. 77.

97 Hayek, p. 77.

98 Hayek, p. 82.

99 Hayek, p. 78.

100 Hayek, p. 83.

101 Hayek, p. 83-84.

102 Hayek, p. 158.

103 Pope Benedict XVI, Encyclical Letter, *Caritas en Veritate*, 34.

104 Fr. Robert Sirico, *Defending the Free Market*, Regnery Publishing, 2012, p. 169.

105 Pope Emeritus Benedict XVI, 6.

106 Gregg, p. 97-98.

107 Pope Pius XI, 58.

108 Pope Pius XI, 22.

109 Pope Pius XI, 4. (attributed to Pope Pius IX)

110 Pope Pius XI, 10.

111 Sirico, p. 33.

112 Pope Leo XIII, 3.

113 Pope Leo XIII, 15.

114 Saint John Paul II, 48.

115 Saint John Paul II, 48.

116 Pope Pius XI, Encyclical Letter *Quadragesimo Anno*, 203, and *Catechism of the Catholic Church*, 1883.

117 Pontifical Council for Justice and Peace, *Compendium of the Social Doctrine of the Church*, Eighth Printing, August 2017, p. 82-83.

118 Pope Benedict XVI, Encyclical Letter *Deus Caritas Est*.

119 Pope Pius XI, Encyclical Letter *Divini Redemptoris*, 32.

120 Pope Pius XI, Encyclical Letter *Divini Redemptoris*, 34.

121 Pope Pius XI, Encyclical Letter *Divini Redemptoris*, 43.

122 Pope Pius XI, Encyclical Letter *Divini Redemptoris*, 43.

123 Saint John Paul II, Encyclical Letter, *Centesimus Annus*, 41.

124 Novak, p. 53.

125 *Compendium*, 347.

126 *Compendium*, 349.

127 *The Catechism of the Catholic Church*, 1807.

128 *Catechism*, 1836.

129 *The Holy Bible* (NIV), Matthew 22:36-40.

130 Saint John Paul II, Encyclical Letter *Centesimus Annus*, 41.

131 *Compendium*, 348.

132 *Vocation of the Business Leader – A Reflection*, Pontifical Council for Justice and Peace, Nov. 2014, 41.

133 *Vocation*, p. 17.

134 *Vocation*, p. 17.

135 *Vocation*, 43.

136 Saint John Paul II, Encyclical Letter *Laborem Exercens*, 6.

137 *Vocation*, 46.

138 *Vocation*, 44.

139 *Vocation*, p. 17.

140 *Vocation*, 46.

141 *Vocation*, 47.

142 *Vocation*, 48.

143 *Vocation*, p. 17.

144 *Vocation*, p. 17.

145 Saint John Paul II, Encyclical Letter *Centesimus Annus*, 35.

146 *Vocation*, 51.

147 *Vocation*, 51.

148 *Vocation*, 51.

149 *Vocation*, p. 17

150 *Vocation*, 56.

151 Pope Pius XI, Encyclical Letter *Quadragesimo Anno*, 72 (paraphrased from).

152 *The Holy Bible* (RSV), Wisdom, 8:7.

153 *Catechism*, 1803.

154 *Catechism*, 1804.

155 Heilbroner, p. 58.

156 *Catechism*, 1811.

157 Pope Leo XIII, Encyclical Letter *Rerum Novarum*, 3.

158 *Catechism*, 1813.

159 *Catechism*, 1806.

160 *Catechism*, 1806.

161 *Catechism*, 1809.

162 *Catechism*, 1807.

163 *Catechism*, 1808.

164 Saint John Paul II, Encyclical Letter *Centesimus Annus*, 35.

165 Saint John Paul II, Encyclical Letter *Centesimus Annus*, 48.

166 Saint John Paul II, Encyclical Letter *Laborem Exercens*, 7.

167 Saint John Paul II, Encyclical Letter *Laborem Exercens*, 7.

168 Saint John Paul II, Encyclical Letter *Laborem Exercens*, 8.

169 Saint John Paul II, Encyclical Letter *Laborem Exercens*, 13.

170 Saint John Paul II, Encyclical Letter *Laborem Exercens*, 17.

171 Saint John Paul II, Encyclical Letter *Laborem Exercens*, 20.

172 Novak, p. 84.

173 Pakaluk, Burke, and Widmer, *Solidarity and Job Creation: Substitutes or Complements?*, June 2014.

174 Pope Pius XI, Encyclical Letter *Quadragesimo Anno*, May 1931, 50-51.

175 Michael Matheson Miller, SAT Talks (The Videos, 2015).

176 *The Holy Bible (RSV)*, Deuteronomy 24:14-15.

177 Gary Hamel, *The Future of Management*, p. 33.

178 *The Holy Bible (NIV)*, Ezekiel 36:26.

179 *The Holy Bible (NIV)*, Luke 16:10.

180 *The Holy Bible (NIV)*, Proverbs 25:22.

Printed in the United States
By Bookmasters